HOW A SUCCESSFUL MINDSET THINKS

ELEVEN SECRETS TO A SUCCESSFUL MINDSET

BY

Prof John Morgan

Copyright @ 2022 Prof John Morgan

All rights reserved

Table of Contents

introduction 3
CHAPTER ONE 5
Developing a successful mindset 5
   Why You Ought to Get THE Insight OF Higher perspective reasoning 8
CHAPTER TWO 13
Taking part in Centered Thinking 13
CHAPTER THREE 22
Bridle Inventive Reasoning 22
   Step by step instructions to find the Delight Of Imaginative Reasoning 27
CHAPTER SIX 34
Utilize Reasonable Reasoning 34
   Why You Ought to Perceive the Significance of Reasonable Reasoning 34
   Instructions to Perceive THE Significance OF Reasonable Reasoning 37
CHAPTER SEVEN 43
Use Key Reasoning 43

PLAN YOUR LIFE, Experience YOUR Arrangement 43

WHY YOU Ought to Delivery THE Force OF Vital Reasoning 44

CHAPTER SEVEN 52

Investigate Plausibility Thinking 52

The most effective method to FEEL THE ENERGY OFPOSSIBILITY THINKING 55

CHAPTER EIGHT 61

Gain from Intelligent Reasoning 61

The most effective method to EMBRACE THE Examples OF Intelligent Reasoning 64

CHAPTER EIGHT 69

Question well known Thinking 69

WHY YOU Ought to Scrutinize The Acknowledgment OF Famous Reasoning 70

Instructions to Scrutinize THE Acknowledgment OF Well known THINKING 73

CHAPTER NINE 78

Benefit from Shared Thinking 78

CHAPTER TEN 86
Practice Unselfish Reasoning 86
   Step by step instructions to EXPERIENCE THE Fulfillment OF UNSELFISH Reasoning 89

CHAPTER ELEVEN 95
Depend on Main concern Thinking 95
   A NONPROFIT'S Main concern 95
   WHY YOU Ought to Partake in THE Arrival OF Primary concern THINKING 97
   Instructions to Partake in THE Arrival OF Primary concern THINKING 99

INTRODUCTION

Great scholars are consistently popular. An individual who realizes how may continuously have some work, yet the individual who realizes the reason why will constantly be his chief. Great scholars take care of issues, they never need thoughts that can assemble an association, and they generally have trust for a superior future. Great masterminds seldom wind up at the leniency of heartless individuals who might exploit them or attempt to mislead them, individuals like Nazi tyrant Adolf

Hitler, who once gloated, "What karma for rulers that men don't think." The individuals who foster the course of good thinking can control themselves — even while under an abusive ruler or in other troublesome conditions. So, great scholars are fruitful.

I've read up effective individuals for a very long time, and however the variety you find among them is surprising, I've observed that they are similar in one manner: their thought process! That is the one thing that isolates fruitful individuals from fruitless ones. Also, here's the uplifting news. Fruitful individuals' thought process can be learned. Assuming you change your reasoning, you can transform you!

CHAPTER ONE

DEVELOPING A SUCCESSFUL MINDSET

"Where achievement is concerned, individuals are not estimated in inches, or pounds, or professional educations, or family foundation; they are estimated by the size of their reasoning."

Successful mindset thinking can help any individual in any calling. At the point when someone like Jack Welch tells a Representative that the continuous relationship with the client is a higher priority than the offer of a person item, he's helping them to remember the successful mindset. At the point when two guardians are tired of potty preparation, terrible scores, or then again minor collisions, and one reminds the other that the ebb and flow troublesome time is just a brief season, then they benefit from dreaming successful mindset. Land designer Donald Trump joked, "You need to think in any case, so why not ignore any perceived limitations?" successful mindset thinking carries completeness and development to an individual's reasoning. It brings point of view. It resembles making the casing of an image greater, in the process growing not just what you can see, in any case, what you can do. Invest energy with successful mindset masterminds, and you will track down that them:

Learn continually

Successful mindset masterminds are forever discontent with what they definitely know. They are continuously visiting new spots, perusing new books, meeting new individuals, acquiring new abilities. Furthermore, in light of that training, they frequently can associate the detached. They are deep rooted students.

To assist me with keeping a student's demeanor, I put shortly each day pondering my learning open doors for the afternoon. As I audit my schedule and daily agenda — knowing whom I will meet that day, what I will peruse, which gatherings I will join in — I note where I'm probably going to learn something. Then I intellectually prompt myself to search mindfully for something that will further develop me in that. On the off chance that you want to continue to learn, I need to urge you to analyze your day and search for chances to learn.

Listen Purposefully

A brilliant method for expanding your experience is to pay attention to somebody who has ability in a space where you don't. I look for such open doors. One year I addressed around 900 mentors and scouts at the Senior Bowl, where graduating football players take part in their last school game. I had the open door, alongside my child in-regulation, Steve Mill operator, to eat with NFL lead trainers Dave Wannstedt and Butch Davis. Rarely would you get such an open door, so I asked them inquiries about cooperation and invested a great deal of energy paying attention to them. Toward the finish of the night, as Steve and I were strolling to our vehicle, he shared with me, "John, I bet you posed those mentors 100 inquiries this evening."

"Assuming I will learn and develop," I answered, "I should understand what inquiries to pose and know how to apply the solutions to my life. Listening has shown me significantly more than talking."

At the point when you meet with individuals, it's great to have a plan so you can learn. It's an extraordinary method for collaborating with individuals who can do things you can't. Higher perspective masterminds perceive that they don't know bunches of things. They habitually pose entering inquiries to extend their comprehension and thinking. To improve as a higher perspective mastermind, then become a decent audience.

Look Expansively

Essayist Henry David Thoreau expressed, "Numerous an article isn't seen, however it falls inside the scope of our visual beam, since it doesn't come quite close to our scholarly beam." Individuals constantly see their own world first. For instance, when individuals show up at an initiative gathering put on by my organization, they need to know where they will stop, whether they will actually want to get a decent (and agreeable) seat, whether the speaker will be "on," and assuming that the breaks will be separated right. At the point when I show up to talk at a similar gathering, I need to realize that the lighting is great, the sound gear is working actually, whether the speaker's stage will be sufficiently close to individuals, and so on. What your identity is figures out what you see — and your thought process.

Higher perspective scholars acknowledge there is a world out there other than their own, and they really try to get beyond themselves and see others' universes through their eyes. Seeing the image while inside is hard the casing. To perceive how others see, you should initially figure out their thought process. Turning into a decent audience positively assists with that. So does moving past your own plan and attempting to take the other individual's point of view.

Live Totally

French writer Michel Eyquem de Montaigne expressed, "The worth of life lies not in that frame of mind of days, but rather in the utilization we make of them; a man might live lengthy yet live very little." truly you can consume your time on earth any way you need, however you can spend it just a single time. Turning into a successful mindset mastermind can assist you with living with completeness, to carry on with a very satisfying life. ?individuals who understand the situation completely extend their experience since they grow their reality. Thus, they achieve more than extremist individuals. What's more, they experience less undesirable astonishments, as well, since they are bound to see the huge number engaged with any given circumstance: issues, individuals, connections, timing, and values. They are likewise, in this way, normally more open minded toward others and their reasoning.

Why You Ought to Get THE Insight OF Higher perspective reasoning

Naturally, you presumably perceive higher perspective reasoning as gainful. Scarcely any individuals need to be shut leaning. Nobody embarks to be like that. Yet, in the event you're not totally persuaded, think about a few explicit motivations behind why you ought to put forth the attempt to improve as a successful mindset scholar:

1. Successful mindset Thinking Permits You to Lead

You can find some higher perspective scholars who aren't pioneers, yet you will find not many pioneers who are not enormous picture masterminds. Pioneers should have the option to do numerous significant things for their kin:

See the vision before their kin do, they likewise see a greater amount of it. This permits them to Size up circumstances, considering numerous factors. Pioneers who understand the situation recognize conceivable outcomes as well as issues to frame an establishment to fabricate the vision. Whenever pioneers have done that, they can Sketch an image of where the group is going, including any expected difficulties or obstructions. The objective of pioneers ought not to be simply to encourage their kin, however to help them be great and achieve the fantasy. The vision, shown precisely, will permit pioneers to Show how what's to come interfaces with the past to make the excursion more significant. At the point when pioneers perceive this requirement for association and extension it, then they can take advantage of the opportunity while the timing is correct. In administration, when to move is just about as significant as what you do. As Winston Churchill said, "There comes an extraordinary second in everybody's life, a second for which that individual was conceived. When he holds onto it… it is his best hour."

Whether building streets, arranging an outing, or moving in initiative, successful mindset thinking permits you to appreciate more achievement. Individuals who are continually taking a gander at the entire picture have the most obvious opportunity with regards to prevailing in any undertaking.

2. successful mindset Thinking Keeps You On track Thomas Fuller, clergyman to Charles II of Britain, noticed, "He that is wherever is no place." To get things done, you really want center. Be that as it may, to finish the right things, you likewise need to think about the successful mindset. Exclusively by placing your everyday exercises with regards to the successful mindset can you stay on track? As According to alvin Toffler, "You must contemplate 'huge things' while you're doing little things, so every one of the little things head down the correct path."

3. Higher perspective Reasoning Permits You to See What Others See Quite possibly of the main expertise you can foster in human relations is the

capacity to see things according to the next individual's perspective. It's one of the keys to working with clients, fulfilling clients, keeping a marriage, raising kids, helping the individuals who are less lucky, and so on. All human communications are improved by the capacity to imagine someone else's perspective. How? Look past yourself, your own advantages, and your own reality. At the point when you work to think about an issue from each conceivable point, look at it in the radiance of another's set of experiences, find the interests and worries of others, and attempt to save your own plan, you start to see what others see. Furthermore, that is something strong.

4. Successful mindset Thinking Advances Cooperation

In the event that you take part in any sort of group movement, you know how significant it is that colleagues understand the situation from start to finish, in addition to their own part. Whenever an individual doesn't have any idea how his work fits with that of his partners, then, at that point, the entire group is in a tough situation. The better the grip colleagues have of the successful mindset, the more noteworthy their capability to cooperate collectively.

5. Higher perspective Reasoning Holds you back from Being Up to speed in the Ordinary Can we just be real: a few parts of day to day existence are totally fundamental yet completely tedious. Enormous picture masterminds don't allow the drudgery to get to them, since they don't fail to focus on the exceptionally significant outline. They realize that the individual who fails to remember a definitive is a captive to the quick.

6. Successful mindset Figuring Assists You with graphing an unfamiliar Area Have you heard the saying, "We'll address that concern when we come to it"? That expression without a doubt was begat by somebody who experienced difficulty understanding the situation. The world was worked by individuals who "crossed spans" to them some time before any other person did. The best way to kick off something new or move into an unknown area is to look past the prompt and understand the situation from start to finish. The most effective method to Gain THE Insight OF Higher perspective Reasoning On the off chance

that you want to quickly jump all over new chances and open new skylines, you really want to add higher perspective thinking to your capacities.

To turn into a decent mastermind better ready to understand the situation completely, remember the accompanying ideas:

1. Try not to take a stab at Sureness

Higher perspective masterminds are alright with vagueness. They don't attempt to drive each perception or piece of information into pre-formed mental cubby openings. They think comprehensively and can shuffle some apparently disconnected contemplations to them. To develop the capacity to dream higher perspective, then, at that point, you should become accustomed to embracing and managing complicated and various thoughts.

2. Gain from Each Insight

Successful mindset scholars expand their standpoint by endeavoring to gain from each insight. They don't lay on their triumphs, they gain from them. All the more significantly, they gain from their disappointments. They can do that since they stay workable.

Changed encounters — both positive and negative — assist you with understanding the situation from start to finish. The more prominent the assortment of involvement and achievement, the more potential to learn you have. In the event that you want to be a successful mindset mastermind, then, at that point, get out there and attempt a ton of things, take a ton of risks, and carve out opportunity to learn after each triumph or rout.

3. Acquire Knowledge from Various Individuals

Successful mindset masterminds gain from their encounters. However, they additionally gain from encounters they don't have. That is, they advance by getting knowledge from others — from clients, representatives, associates, and pioneers.

Assuming you want to expand your reasoning and see a greater amount of the higher perspective, then search out guides to help you. In any case, be astute in whom you request exhortation. Acquiring knowledge from different individuals doesn't mean halting everybody in lobbies and supermarket lines and getting some information about a given subject. Be specific. Converse with individuals who know and care about you, who know their field, and who bring experience further and more extensive than your own.

4. Allow Yourself to Grow Your Reality

To be a successful mindset mastermind, you should run contrary to current trend of the world. Society needs to keep individuals in boxes. A great many people are hitched intellectually to the state of affairs. They need what was, not what can be. They look for security and straightforward responses. To dream higher perspective, you really want to allow yourself to go an alternate way, to kick off something new, to track down new universes to win. Furthermore, when your reality gets greater, you really want to celebrate. Always remember there is more out there on the planet than what you've encountered.

Continue learning, continue developing, and continue to take a gander at the higher perspective; In the event that you want to be a decent mastermind, which is the thing you want to do.

Thinking Question

Am I thinking past myself and my reality so I process thoughts with a comprehensive perspective?

CHAPTER TWO

TAKING PART IN CENTERED THINKING

"He did everything as though he did nothing else."

Scholar Bertrand Russell once declared, "To have the option to think for a significant time frame is vital for troublesome accomplishment." Humanist Robert Lynd saw that "information is power provided that a man understands what realities are not to fret over." Centered speculation eliminates interruptions and mental mess so you can focus on an issue and think with clearness. Centered speculation can complete a few things for you:

1. Centered Speculation Outfits Energy toward an Ideal Objective

Center can carry energy and capacity to nearly anything, whether physical or mental. In the event that you're figuring out how to throw a baseball and you need to foster a decent curve, then engaged thinking while at the same time rehearsing will get to the next level your procedure. On the off chance that you really want to refine the assembling system of your item, engaged speculation will help you foster the best strategy. If you have any desire to tackle a troublesome science issue, centered speculation assists you with breaking through to the arrangement. The more prominent the trouble of an issue or issue, the more engaged speculation time is important to tackle it.

2. Centered Speculation Gives Thoughts Time to Create

I love to find and foster thoughts. I frequently unite my imaginative group for conceptualizing and inventive reasoning. At the point when we initially get together, we attempt to be comprehensive in our reasoning to create however many thoughts as could be allowed. The birthing of a potential advancement frequently comes about because of sharing numerous smart thoughts.

Yet, to take thoughts to a higher level, you should move from being sweeping in your reasoning to being specific. I have found that a smart thought can turn into a good thought when it is given center time. It is actually the case that zeroing in on a solitary thought for quite a while can very disappoint. I've frequently gone through days zeroing in on an idea and attempting to foster it, just to find that I was unable to work on the thought. Yet, now and again my diligence in centered thinking pays off. That gives me incredible pleasure. What's more, while centered believing is at its ideal, besides the fact that the thought develops, yet so do I!

3. Centered Speculation Carries Lucidity to the Objective

I think about golf one of my #1 leisure activities. It's a brilliantly difficult game. I like it on the grounds that the targets are so clear. Teacher William Mobley of the College of South Carolina mentioned the accompanying objective fact about golf:

Perhaps of the main thing about golf is the presence of clear objectives. You see the pins, you know the standard — it's neither too simple nor unreachable, you know your typical score, and there are cutthroat objectives — serious with standard, with yourself as well as other people.

These objectives give you something to take shots at. In work, as in golf, objectives rouse.

Once on the fairway, I followed a golf player who failed to return the pin to the opening after he putted. Since I was unable to see my objective, I was unable to concentrate appropriately. My concentrate immediately went to dissatisfaction — and to unfortunate play. To be a decent golf player, an individual requirements to zero in on an unmistakable objective. The equivalent is valid in thinking. Center assists you with knowing the objective — and to accomplish it.

4. Centered Speculation Will Take You to A higher Level

Nobody accomplishes significance by turning into a generalist. You don't level up an ability by weakening your regard for its turn of events. The best way to get to a higher level is to center. Regardless of whether you want to expand your degree of play, hone your marketable strategy, work on your main concern, foster your subordinates, or settle individual issues, you want to center. Creator Harry A. Overstreet noticed, "The juvenile psyche jumps starting with one thing then onto the next; the developed brain looks to see everything through to completion."

Where would it be advisable for you to concentrate your thinking?

Does each part of your life merit devoted, centered speculation time? Obviously, the response is no. Be specific, not comprehensive, in your engaged reasoning. As far as I might be concerned, that implies committing top to bottom reasoning chance to four regions: administration, inventiveness, correspondence, and deliberate systems administration. Your decisions will presumably contrast from mine. The following are a couple of ideas to assist you with sorting them out:

Distinguish Your Needs

To start with, consider your needs — for your purposes, your family, and your group. Creator, specialist, and grant winning mastermind Edward DeBono joked, "An end is where you become weary of reasoning." Sadly, many individuals land on needs founded on where they hit a dead end.

You surely don't have any desire to do that. Nor would you like to allow others to set your plan.

There are numerous ways of deciding needs. On the off chance that you realize yourself well, start by zeroing in on your assets, the things that utilize your abilities and inherent gifts. You could likewise zero in on what brings the best yield and prize. Do what you appreciate most and do best. You could utilize the 80/20 rule. Give 80% of your work to the main 20% (generally significant) exercises. Another way is to zero in on extraordinary potential open doors that guarantee a colossal return. All that ultimately matters is this: concentrate entirely on the areas that prove to be fruitful.

Find Your Gifts

Not all individuals are mindful and have a decent handle on their own abilities, gifts, and abilities. They are a bit like the funny cartoon character Charlie Brown. One day in the wake of striking out in a ball game, he says, "Rodents! I'll never be a major association player. I simply don't have it! For my entire life I've longed for playing in the major associations, yet I'll never make it."

To which Lucy answers, "Charlie Brown, you're thinking excessively far ahead. What you really want to do is defined more quick objectives for yourself."

Briefly, Charlie Earthy colored sees a beam of trust. "Quick objectives?" he says.

"Indeed," answers Lucy. "Begin with the following inning. At the point when you go out to pitch, check whether you can leave to the hill without tumbling down!"

I've met numerous people who experienced childhood in a family brimming with Lucy. They got little support or confirmation, and therefore appear to be confused for course. Assuming you have that sort of foundation, you really want to work extra difficult to sort out what your gifts are. Take a character profile like Plate or Myers-Briggs. Interview positive loved ones to see where they think you sparkle. Invest some energy thinking about past triumphs. In the event that you will concentrate your reasoning in your solid areas, you want to understand what they are.

Foster Your Fantasy

To accomplish incredible things, you want to have an extraordinary dream. In the event that you don't know of your fantasy, utilize your engaged reasoning chance to assist you with finding it. On the off chance that your reasoning has gotten back to a specific region many times, you might have the option to find your fantasy there. Give it more engaged time and see what occurs. When you track down your fantasy, push ahead without rethinking. Take the guidance of Travel bag Paige: "Don't think back — something may be acquiring on you."

The more youthful you are, the almost certain you will concentrate on numerous things. That is great since, supposing that you're youthful you're actually getting to know yourself, your assets and shortcomings. Assuming you center you're reasoning around just something single and your goals change, then you've squandered your best mental energy. As you age and more encountered, the need to concentrate turns out to be more basic. The farther and higher you go, the more engaged you can be — and should be.

How Might You Keep on Track?

When you have an idea about what you ought to think about, you should choose how to more readily zero in on it. The following are five ideas to assist you with the cycle:

1. Eliminate Interruptions

Eliminating interruptions is no little matter in our ongoing society, yet entirely it's basic. How would you make it happen? In the first place, by keeping up with the discipline of rehearsing your needs. Try not to do simple things first or hard things first or dire things first. Do priorities straight — the exercises that give you the best yield. In like that, you keep the interruptions to a base.

Second, protect yourself from interruptions. I've found that I really want blocks of time to think without interferences. I've become amazing at making myself inaccessible when fundamental and heading out to my "thinking place" so I can work without interferences. As a result of my obligations as organizer behind three organizations, be that as it may, I'm dependably mindful of the pressure between my need to stay open to others as a pioneer and my need to pull out from them to think. The most effective way to determine the pressure is to figure out the worth of the two exercises. Strolling gradually through the group permits me to interface with individuals and know their requirements.

Pulling out from the group permits me to consider ways of enhancing them. My recommendation to you is to put esteem on and concentrate completely on both. On the off chance that you normally pull out, make a point to get out among individuals on a more regular basis. On the off chance that you're dependably in a hurry and seldom pull out for thinking time, eliminate yourself intermittently so you can release the capability of centered thinking. Also, any place you are… be there!

2. Set aside a few minutes for Centered Thinking

When you have a spot to think, you really want an opportunity to think. Due to the high speed of our way of life, individuals tend to perform multiple tasks. Yet, that is not generally smart. Changing from one errand to another can cost you up to 40 percent productivity. As per scientists, "On the off chance that you're attempting to get numerous things done simultaneously, you'll get more finished by zeroing in on each undertaking in turn, not by exchanging continually starting with one assignment then onto the next."

Quite back I understood that my best reasoning time happens in the first part of the day. Whenever the situation allows, I save my mornings for thinking and composing. One method for acquiring time for centered believing is to force upon yourself a standard that one organization carried out. Try not to permit yourself to see email until after E0 A.M. All things being equal, center your energies on your main need. Put non-useful time killers on pause so you can make thinking time for yourself.

3. Keep Things of Concentration before You

Ralph Waldo Emerson, the extraordinary supernatural scholar, accepted, "Fixation is the mystery of solidarity in legislative issues, in battle, in exchange, in short in all administration of human undertakings." To assist me with focusing on the things that matter, I work to keep significant things before me. One way is to ask my partner, Linda Eggers, to keep bringing it up, getting some information about it, giving me extra data concerning it.

I'll likewise keep a record or a page directly in front of me so I see it consistently as I work. That technique has effectively helped me for a very long time to invigorate and hone thoughts. Assuming you've never gotten it done, I suggest that you attempt it. (I'll educate you more in the part on intelligent reasoning.)

4. Put forth Objectives

I accept objectives are significant. The brain won't concentrate until it has clear goals. However, the reason for objectives is to concentrate and provide you guidance, not to recognize a last objective. As you ponder your objectives, note that they ought to be.

- Adequately clear to be maintained in center
- Sufficiently close to be accomplished
- Adequately accommodating to change lives

Those rules will get you moving. What's more, make certain to record your objectives. On the off chance that they're not composed, I can nearly ensure that they're not adequately centered.

What's more, to ensure they're engaged, take the exhortation of David Belasco, who says, "In the event that you can't compose your thought on the rear of my business card, you don't have a clear thought."

Regardless of whether you think back a very long time from now and think your objectives were excessively little, they will have filled their need — in the event that they give you course.

5. Question Your Advancement

Look closely at yourself occasionally to see whether you are really gaining ground. That is the most exact proportion of whether you are utilizing centered thinking. Ask yourself, "Am I seeing a return for my venture of centered speculation time? Is the thing I'm doing drawing me nearer to my objectives? Am I traveled toward a path that assists me with satisfying my responsibilities, keep up with my needs, and understand my fantasies?"

What are you Surrendering Doing GO?

Nobody can go to the most significant level and stay a generalist. My father used to say, "Find the one thing you do well and do nothing else." I've found that to find real success at a couple of things, I have needed to surrender numerous things. As I chipped away at this part, I invested some energy thinking about the sorts of things I've surrendered. Here are the fundamental ones:

I Can't Know Everybody

I love individuals, and I'm cordial. Put me into a room brimming with individuals, and I feel stimulated. So it conflicts with my grain to confine myself from investing energy with heaps of individuals. To make up for that, I've done two or three things. To begin with, I've picked areas of strength for a circle of individuals. They not just give enormous expert assistance, yet, they likewise make life's excursion significantly more wonderful. Second, I request that specific companions get me up on what's occurring in the existences of different companions. I normally do that while I'm voyaging and can't shut out the time I would need for centered thinking.

I Can't Do Everything

There are a couple of remarkable open doors in any individual's lifetime. That is the reason I make progress toward greatness in a couple of things as opposed to a decent presentation in many. That is set me back. Due to my responsibility, I likewise need to skip doing numerous things that I couldn't want anything more than to do. For instance, consistently I hand off projects that I think would be enjoyable to do myself. I practice the E0-80-E0 standard with individuals to whom I'm designating an undertaking. I assist with the principal E0 percent by projecting vision, setting down boundaries, giving assets, and giving support. Then whenever they've done the center 80%, I come close by them once more and assist them with taking anything it is the remainder of the way, on the off chance that I can. I call it putting the clincher.

I Can't Go All over

Each meeting speaker and creator needs to travel a ton. Before I started doing a lot talking, that appeared like a spectacular life. Yet, subsequent to logging a few million miles, I understand what sort of a cost it can take. Amusingly, I still love going for joy with my significant other, Margaret. It's one of our extraordinary delights. She and I could take ten get-away a year and partake in all of them. However we can't, on the grounds that such a large amount my time is consumed doing what I was called to do: assist individuals with developing by and by and to create as pioneers.

I Can't Be Well2Rounded

Being centered likewise holds me back from being balanced. I tell individuals, "the vast majority of everything in life I don't have to be aware of." I attempt to zero in on the one percent that gives the best yield. Furthermore, of the staying 99, Margaret keeps me mindful of anything that I want to be aware. It's one of the manners in which I hold back from getting thoroughly out of equilibrium in my life.

Being willing to surrender a portion of the things you love to zero in on what has the best effect is certainly not a simple example to learn. Yet, the previous you embrace it, the sooner you can devote yourself to greatness in what makes the biggest difference.

Thinking Question

Am I devoted to eliminating interruptions and mental mess so I can focus with clarity on the main problem?

CHAPTER THREE

BRIDLE INVENTIVE REASONING

"The delight is in making, not keeping up with."

Inventiveness is unadulterated gold, regardless of how you make ends meet. Annette Moser-Wellman, creator of The Five Appearances of Virtuoso, declares, "The most significant asset you bring to your work and to your firm is your innovativeness.

More than what you finish, more than the job you play, more than your title, more than your 'yield' — it's your thoughts that matter." 3 In spite of the significance of an individual's capacity to think with imagination, hardly any individuals appear to have the expertise in overflow.

In the event that you're not as imaginative as you might want to be, you can impact your perspective. Innovative reasoning isn't really unique reasoning. I think individuals mythologize unique idea, as a matter of fact. Most frequently, inventive reasoning is a composite of different considerations found en route. Indeed, even the extraordinary craftsmen, whom we consider exceptionally unique, gained from their lords, demonstrated their work on that of others, and united a large group of thoughts and styles to make their own work. Concentrate on craftsmanship, and you will see strings that go through crafted by all specialists and imaginative developments, interfacing them to different specialists who went before them.

Qualities of Imaginative Masterminds

Maybe you're not even certain what I mean when I find out if you are an inventive mastermind. Consider a few qualities that imaginative scholars share for all intents and purpose:

Inventive Masterminds worth Thoughts

Annette Moser-Wellman notices, "Exceptionally innovative individuals are committed to thoughts. They don't depend on their ability alone; they depend on their discipline. Their creative mind resembles a subsequent skin. They know how to control it to its fullest." 4 Imagination is tied in with having thoughts — bunches of them. You will have thoughts provided that you esteem thoughts.

Inventive Masterminds Investigate Choices

I've yet to meet an inventive mastermind who didn't cherish choices. Investigating a large number of potential outcomes serves to animate the creative mind, and creative mind is essential to inventiveness. As Albert Einstein put it, "Creative mind is a higher priority than information."

Individuals who realize me well will let you know that I put an extremely high worth on choices. Why? Since they give the way to tracking down the most fitting response — not by any means the only response. Great scholars think of the most intelligent responses. They make fall backs that furnish them with choices. They appreciate opportunity that others don't have. Also, they will impact and lead others.

Innovative Scholars Embrace Uncertainty

Essayist H. L. Mencken said, "The dull man is in every case sure, and the definite man who is generally dull."

Imaginative individuals don't want to get rid of vulnerability. They see a wide range of irregularities and holes throughout everyday life, and they frequently take savor the experience of investigating those holes — or in utilizing their creative mind to fill them in.

Innovative Scholars Commend the Strange

Innovativeness, by its actual nature, frequently investigates off of the most common way to go and runs contrary to the natural order of things. Representative and long-term leader of Yale College Kingman Brewster said, "There is a relationship between the innovative and the screwball. So we should experience the screwball happily." To encourage imagination in yourself or others, endure a little peculiarity.

Inventive Scholars Interface the Detached

Since imagination uses the thoughts of others, there's extraordinary worth in having the option to associate one plan to another — particularly to apparently inconsequential thoughts. According to visual originator Tim Hansen, "Inventiveness is particularly communicated in the capacity to make associations, to make relationship, to make something happen and communicate them in another way."

Making extra contemplations resembles going on an outing in your vehicle. You might know where you are going, yet just as may be obvious and experience things in a manner unrealistic before you began. Imaginative reasoning works something like this:

 THINK _ Gather _ Make _ Right _ Interface

When you start to think, you are allowed to gather. You ask yourself, what material connects with this idea?

When you have the material, you ask, what thoughts can improve the idea? That can begin to take a thought to a higher level. From that point onward, you can address or refine it by asking, what changes can improve these thoughts?

At long last, you associate the thoughts by situating them in the right setting to make the idea complete and strong.

Imaginative Masterminds Don't Dread Disappointment

Innovativeness requests the capacity to be unafraid of disappointment since imagination rises to disappointment. You might be shocked to hear such a proclamation, yet all the same it's valid. Charles Frankel declares that "tension is the fundamental condition of scholarly and imaginative creation." Inventiveness requires an eagerness to look dumb. It implies getting out on an appendage — realizing that the appendage frequently breaks! Innovative individuals know these things nevertheless continue to look for new thoughts. They simply don't let the thoughts that don't work keep them from thinking of additional thoughts that take care of business.

Why you ought to find THE Delight OF Imaginative Reasoning

Innovativeness can further develop an individual's personal satisfaction. The following are five explicit things imaginative reasoning can possibly accomplish for you:

1. Inventive Reasoning Increases the value of everything

Couldn't you partake in a boundless repository of thoughts that you could draw upon out of the blue? That is what innovative thinking gives you. Therefore, regardless of what you are at present ready to do, innovativeness can expand your capacities.

Inventiveness is having the option to see what every other person has seen and think what no other person has thought with the goal that you can do what no other individual has done. Some of the time imaginative reasoning lies as per innovation, where you kick off something new. Different times it moves as per development, which assists you with doing old things in another manner. Yet, one way or the other, it's seeing the world through adequately new eyes so new arrangements show up. That generally adds esteem.

2. Inventive Reasoning Mixtures

Throughout the long term, I've seen that as Inventive Reasoning Is Difficult Work be that as it may Inventive Reasoning Mixtures adequately given Time and Concentration Maybe more than some other perspective, inventive reasoning expands on itself and builds the imagination of the scholar. Writer Maya Angelou noticed, "You can't go through innovativeness. The more you use, the more you have.

Unfortunately, again and again innovativeness is covered as opposed to supported. There must be an environment in which better approaches for thinking, seeing, addressing are energized." Assuming you develop imaginative reasoning in a climate that sustains imagination, it's impossible to tell what sort of thoughts you can concoct. (I'll talk inclining further toward that later.)

3. Innovative Reasoning Attracts Individuals to You and You're Thoughts

Imagination is knowledge having some good times. Individuals appreciate knowledge, and they are constantly drawn to fun — so the mix is phenomenal. In the event that anybody could be said to play around with his knowledge, it was Leonardo da Vinci.

The variety of his thoughts and aptitude stuns the brain. He was a painter, modeler, stone worker, anatomist, artist, creator, and architect. The term Renaissance man was instituted as a result of him.

Similarly as individuals were attracted to Da Vinci and his thoughts during the Renaissance, they are attracted to imaginative individuals today. On the off chance that you develop innovativeness, you will turn out to be more alluring to others, and they will be attracted to you.

4. Inventive Reasoning assists you with finding out more

Creator and innovativeness master Ernie Zelinski says, "Imagination is the delight of not knowing everything. The delight of not realizing everything alludes to the acknowledgment that we sometimes if at any point have every one of the responses; we generally can produce more answers for pretty much any issue. Being innovative is having the option to see or envision an extraordinary arrangement of chance to life's concerns. Inventiveness is having choices."

It nearly appears to be too clear to even think about saying, yet on the off chance that you are in every case effectively looking for novel thoughts, you will learn.

Inventiveness is openness to instruction. It's seeing a bigger number of arrangements than issues. What's more, the more prominent the amount of contemplations, the more prominent the opportunity for discovering some new information.

5. Inventive Reasoning Stirs things up

Assuming you want to work on your reality — or even your own circumstance — then, at that point, inventiveness will help you. Business as usual and innovativeness are contradictory. Imagination and development generally walk inseparably.

Step by step instructions to find the Delight Of Imaginative Reasoning

As of now you might say, "Alright, I'm persuaded that inventive reasoning is significant. Be that as it may, how would I track down the innovativeness inside me? How would I find the delight of innovative idea?" The following are five methods for making it happen:

1. Eliminate Imagination Executioners

Financial aspects teacher and humor writer Stephen Leacock said, "By and by, I would sooner have composed Alice in Wonderland than the entire Reference book Britannica." He esteemed the glow of inventiveness over cool realities. In the event that you do as well, you want to kill mentalities that depreciate imaginative reasoning.

Investigate the accompanying expressions. They are nearly ensured to kill innovative reasoning any time you hear (or think) them:

- I'm Not an Imaginative Individual Keep the Guidelines
- Try not to Get clarification on some pressing issues
- Try not to Appear as something else
- Remain Inside the Lines
- There Is Just a single Way
- Try not to Be Silly
- Be Useful
- Be Serious
- Consider Your Picture
- That is Not Coherent
- It's Not Commonsense
- It's Never Been Finished
- It Isn't possible
- It Didn't Work for Them
- We Attempted That Previously
- It's An excess of Work
- We Can't Bear to Commit an Error
- It Will Be Too Difficult to Even think about directing
- We Lack opportunity and willpower

- We Don't Have the Cash
- Indeed, But
- Play Is Unimportant
- Disappointment Is Conclusive

On the off chance that you assume you have a good thought, don't allow anybody to work you out of it regardless of whether it sounds stupid. Try not to let yourself or any other person subject you to innovativeness executioners. All things considered, you can't venture out and energizing on the off chance that you compel yourself to remain in the standard, worn out groove. Try not to simply work harder at business as usual. Roll out an improvement.

2. Think Inventively by Posing the Right Inquiries

Innovativeness is generally an issue of posing the right inquiries. The board mentor Sir Antony Jay said, "The uncreative brain can recognize wrong responses, however it takes an imaginative psyche to detect wrong inquiries." Wrong questions shut down the course of imaginative reasoning. They direct masterminds down the normal, worn out way, or they scold them into accepting that believing isn't required in any way. To invigorate imaginative reasoning, ask yourself questions such as

- For what reason must it be done along these lines?
- What is the foundational issue?
- What are the basic issues?
- What does this help me to remember?
- What is the inverse?
- What analogy or image assists with making sense of it? For what reason is it significant?
- What's the hardest or most expensive method for getting it done? Who has an alternate point of view on this?
- What occurs on the off chance that we don't do it by any stretch of the imagination?

You understand — and you can presumably concoct better inquiries yourself. Physicist Tom Hirschfield noticed, "On the off chance that you don't ask, 'Why this?' frequently enough, someone will ask, 'Why you?'" If you need to think imaginatively, you should pose great inquiries. You should challenge the interaction.

3. Foster an Imaginative Climate

Charlie Brower said, "A groundbreaking thought is fragile. It very well may be killed by a scoff or a yawn; it tends to be cut to passing by a joke and stressed to death by a dislike the perfect man's forehead." Negative conditions kill huge number of extraordinary thoughts consistently.

An imaginative climate, then again, becomes like a nursery where thoughts get cultivated, sprout up, furthermore, and prosper. An innovative climate:

Supports Innovativeness: David Slopes expresses, "Investigations of imagination recommend that the greatest single variable of whether workers will be inventive is whether they see they have consent." When advancement and very smart are straightforwardly empowered and compensated, then, at that point, individuals see that they have authorization to be innovative. Puts a High Worth in Trust among Colleagues and Distinction: Imagination generally gambles disappointment. That is the reason trust means a lot to imaginative individuals. In the inventive strategy, trust comes from individuals cooperating, from realizing that individuals in the group have experience sending off effective, inventive thoughts, and from the confirmation that innovative thoughts will not go to squander, in light of the fact that they will be carried out.

Embraces the individuals Who Are Innovative: Imaginative individuals commend the unique. How could inventive individuals be dealt with? I take the guidance of Tom Peters: "Remove the numbskulls — support the nuts!" I do that by investing energy with them, which I appreciate in any case. I particularly prefer to maneuver individuals into meetings to generate new ideas. Individuals anticipate a solicitation to such gatherings in light of the fact that the time will be loaded up with energy, thoughts, and chuckling. Furthermore, the chances are high that another task, class, or business technique will result. At the point when that occurs, they likewise realize a party's coming!

Centers around Development, Not Simply Innovation: Sam Weston, maker of the famous activity figure GI Joe, said, "Genuinely pivotal thoughts are interesting, however you don't be guaranteed to require one to make a vocation out of inventiveness. My meaning of inventiveness is the coherent mix of at least two existing components that outcome in another idea. The most effective way to earn enough to pay the bills with your creative mind is to create imaginative applications, not envision totally new ideas." Imaginative individuals say, "Give me a smart thought and I'll give you a superior thought!" Will Allow Individuals to go External the Lines: A great many people naturally stay inside lines, regardless of whether those lines have been randomly coaxed or are horribly obsolete. Keep in mind, most impediments we face are not forced on us by others; we put them on ourselves. Absence of inventiveness frequently falls into that class. If you have any desire to be more inventive, challenge limits. Innovator Charles Kettering said, "All human turn of events, regardless of what structure it takes, should be outside the guidelines; any other way, we couldn't have ever anything new." That's what an inventive climate considers.

Values the Force of a Fantasy: An imaginative climate advances the opportunity of a fantasy. An imaginative climate energizes the utilization of a clear piece of paper and the inquiry, "In the event that we could draw an image of what we need to achieve, what might that resemble?" An imaginative climate permitted Martin Luther Lord, Jr., to talk with energy and pronounce to millions, "I have a fantasy," not "I have an objective." Objectives might give concentrate, yet dreams give power. Dreams grow the world. To that end James Allen proposed that "visionaries are the guardian angels of the world."

The greater imagination accommodating you can make your current circumstance, the more potential it needs to become inventive.

4. Invest Energy with Other Imaginative Individuals

Consider the possibility that the spot you work has a climate threatening to innovativeness, and you have little capacity to transform it. One chance is to change occupations. In any case, imagine a scenario where you want to continue to work there in spite of the negative climate? Your most ideal choice is to figure out how to invest energy with other innovative individuals.

Innovativeness is infectious. Have you at any point saw what occurs during a decent meeting to generate new ideas? One individual tosses out a thought. Someone else involves it as a springboard to find another thought. Another person takes it in one more, far and away superior heading. Then someone grasps it and takes it to an unheard of level. The exchange of thoughts can be electric.

I have areas of strength for inventive people in my day to day existence. I try to invest normal energy with them. At the point when I leave them, I generally feel stimulated, I'm loaded with thoughts, and I see things in an unexpected way. They genuinely are key to my life.

It's undeniably truth that you start to think like individuals you invest a great deal of energy with. The additional time you can enjoy with imaginative individuals participating in innovative exercises, the more innovative you will turn into.

5. Escape Your 4ox

Entertainer Katharine Hepburn commented, "Assuming that you submit to all the rules you will miss all the tomfoolery." While I don't believe it's important to defy every one of the guidelines (many are set up to safeguard us), I in all actuality do believe it's hasty to permit purposeful limits to block us. Imaginative masterminds realize that they should more than once break out of the "container" of their own set of experiences and individual impediments to encounter innovative forward leaps.

The best method for assisting yourself with escaping the case is to open yourself to new ideal models. One way you can do that is by going to new spots. Investigate different societies, nations, and customs. Figure out how individuals totally different from you live and think. Another is to peruse on new subjects. I'm normally inquisitive and very much want to learn, yet I actually tend to peruse books just on my number one subjects, like administration. I once in a while need to compel myself to peruse books that widen my reasoning, since I know it's worth the effort. If you have any desire to break out of your own container, get into another person's. Peruse comprehensively.

Many individuals erroneously trust that on the off chance that people aren't brought into the world with imagination, they won't ever be innovative. However, you can see from the numerous systems and models I've given that imagination can be developed in the right steady climate.

Thinking Question

Am I attempting to break out of my "case" of restrictions so I investigate thoughts and choices to encounter innovative breakthroughs?

CHAPTER FOUR

UTILIZE REASONABLE REASONING

"The principal obligation of a pioneer is to characterize reality.

As anybody probably is aware who's been out of school for a couple of years, there's normally an immense hole between an advanced degree and the truth of the functioning scene. Truly, from the get-go in my profession, I made a special effort to stay away from a lot of practical reasoning since I figured it would disrupt my imaginative reasoning. However, as I've developed, I've come to understand that sensible reasoning adds to my life.

Rude awakening

The truth is the contrast between what we wish for and what is. It required an investment for me to develop into a practical mastermind. The cycle went in stages. In the first place, I didn't participate in reasonable reasoning by any means. Sooner or later, I understood that it was fundamental, so I started to once in a while participate in it. (In any case, I could have done without it since I thought it was excessively negative. Furthermore, any time I could appoint it, I did.) Ultimately, I found that I needed to participate in sensible supposing assuming I planned to tackle issues and gain from my missteps. Also, in time, I became able to think practically before I caused problems and make it a consistent piece of my life. Today, I urge my vital chiefs to think everything being equal. We make reasonable reasoning the groundwork of our business since we infer conviction and security from it.

Why You Ought to Perceive the Significance of Reasonable Reasoning

On the off chance that you're a normally hopeful individual, as I'm, you may not have incredible longing to turn into a more sensible scholar. Be that as it may, developing the capacity to be sensible in your reasoning won't sabotage your confidence in individuals, nor will it decrease your capacity to see and take advantage of chances. All things being equal, it will enhance you in alternate ways:

1. Sensible Reasoning Limits Disadvantage Hazard

Activities generally have results; practical reasoning assists you with figuring out what those outcomes could be. Also, that is critical, in light of the fact that simply by perceiving and taking into account results might you at any point plan for them. Assuming you plan for the worst situation imaginable, you can limit the disadvantage risk.

2. Practical Reasoning Gives You an Objective and Strategy

I've known money managers who were not sensible scholars. Here is the uplifting news: they were extremely sure furthermore, had a serious level of expectation for their business. Here is the terrible information: trust isn't a procedure.

Sensible reasoning prompts greatness in administration and the executives since it expects individuals to confront reality. They start to characterize their objective and foster a strategy to hit it. At the point when individuals participate in reasonable reasoning, they additionally start to improve on practices and techniques, which brings about improved proficiency.

Honestly, in business a couple of choices are significant. Practical scholars figure out the distinction between the significant choices and those that are just vital in the typical course of business. The choices that matter relate straightforwardly to your motivation. James Allen was correct when he expressed, "Until believed is connected with reason there is no canny achievement."

3. Reasonable Reasoning Is an Impetus for Change

Individuals who depend on trust for their prosperity seldom focus on change. On the off chance that you have just expectation, you infer that accomplishment and achievement are no longer any of your concern. It's a question of karma or possibility. What is the point of evolving?

Practical reasoning can dissipate that sort of off-base disposition. There's nothing similar to looking straight at reality to cause an individual to perceive the requirement for change. Change alone doesn't bring development however you can't have development without change.

4. Practical Reasoning Gives Security

Any time you have thoroughly considered the most terrible that can occur and you have created alternate courses of action to meet it, you become more certain and secure. It's consoling to realize that you are probably not going to be amazed.

Frustration is the contrast among assumptions and reality. Sensible reasoning limits the distinction between the two.

5. Practical Reasoning Gives You Validity

Practical reasoning assists individuals with purchasing in to the pioneer and their vision. Pioneers persistently astounded by the startling before long lose believability with their devotees. Then again, pioneers who think everything being equal and plan in like manner position their associations to win. That gives their kin trust in them.

The best chiefs pose sensible inquiries prior to projecting vision. They ask themselves things like…

Is it conceivable?

Does this fantasy incorporate everybody or only a couple?

Have I recognized and enunciated the regions that will make this fantasy challenging to accomplish?

6. Sensible Reasoning Gives an Establishment to Expand On

Thomas Edison noticed, "The worth of a smart thought is in utilizing it." The main concern on sensible reasoning is that it assists you with making a thought usable by removing the "wish" factor. Most thoughts and endeavors don't achieve their planned outcomes since they depend a lot on what we wish instead of what is.

You can't fabricate a house in midair; it needs a strong groundwork. Thoughts and plans are something similar. They need something concrete on which to construct. Sensible reasoning gives that strong groundwork.

7. Sensible Reasoning Is a Companion to Those in a difficult situation

Assuming inventiveness is what you would do on the off chance that you were unafraid of the chance of disappointment, the truth is managing disappointment assuming that it works out. Practical reasoning gives you something cement to return to during difficult situations, which can very console. Assurance amidst vulnerability brings soundness.

8. Practical Reasoning Carries the Fantasy to Completion

English writer John Galsworthy stated, "Vision expansions in direct extent to one's separation from the issue." On the off chance that you don't draw near enough to an issue, you can't handle it. In the event that you don't investigate your fantasy — and what it will take to achieve it — you won't ever accomplish it. Sensible reasoning assists with preparing for carrying any fantasy to completion.

Instructions to Perceive THE Significance OF Reasonable Reasoning

Since I'm normally hopeful as opposed to practical, I've needed to find substantial ways to work on my reasoning around here. The following are five things I do to work on my practical reasoning:

1. Foster an Appreciation for Truth

I was unable to create as a practical mastermind until I acquired an appreciation for sensible reasoning. Furthermore, that implies figuring out how to check out and appreciate truth. President Harry S. Truman said, "I never demolish them. I simply come clean and they think it is damnation." That is the manner in which many individuals respond to truth. Individuals will more often than not overstate their prosperity and limit their disappointments or inadequacies. They live as per Ruckert's Regulation, accepting there isn't anything little to the point that it can't be dramatically overemphasized.

Sadly, many individuals today could be portrayed by a statement from Winston Churchill: "Men incidentally stagger over reality, yet most get themselves and rush off as though nothing has occurred." All the more as of late, TV columnist

Ted Koppel noticed, "Our general public views truth as too solid a medication to process undiluted. In its most flawless structure, truth is certainly not a courteous tap on the shoulder. It is a yelling rebuke." all in all, reality will liberate you — however first it will drive you mad! If you have any desire to turn into a practical mastermind, notwithstanding, you want to settle in managing reality and face ready.

2. Get Your Work done

The course of practical reasoning starts with getting your work done. You should initially get current realities. Previous lead representative, senator, and envoy Chester Bowles said, "When you approach an issue, strip yourself of biased suppositions and bias, collect and gain proficiency with current realities of the circumstance, pursue the choice which appears to you in all honestly, and afterward stick to it." It doesn't make any difference how sound your reasoning is assuming it's in view of defective information or presumptions. You can't think well in that frame of mind of realities (or within the sight of poor data).

You can likewise figure out what others have done in comparable conditions. Keep in mind, your reasoning doesn't be guaranteed to must be unique; it simply must be strong. Why not advance all that you can from great scholars who have confronted comparative circumstances before? A portion of my best reasoning has been finished by others!

3. Thoroughly consider the Advantages and disadvantages

There's nothing similar to carving out opportunity to sincerely look at the upsides and downsides of an issue to give you a solid portion of the real world. It seldom boils down to just picking the strategy with the best number of experts, since all advantages and disadvantages don't convey equivalent weight. In any case, that is not the worth of the activity, at any rate. Rather, it assists you with diving into current realities, inspect an issue from many points, and truly consider the consequence of a potential strategy.

4. Picture the Worst2Case Situation

The substance of reasonable reasoning is finding, envisioning, and analyzing the direst outcome imaginable. Ask yourself inquiries, for example, consider the possibility that deals miss the mark regarding projections.

Consider the possibility that income winds up in an almost impossible situation. (Not a confident person's absolute bottom, yet genuine absolute bottom!) Imagine a scenario in which we don't win the record.

Imagine a scenario where the client doesn't pay us.

Imagine a scenario where we need to finish the work under-staffed. Consider the possibility that our best player becomes ill.

Consider the possibility that every one of the schools reject my application. Imagine a scenario where the market kicks the bucket.

Imagine a scenario where the workers quit.

Imagine a scenario where no one appears.

You understand. The fact of the matter is that you want to contemplate most pessimistic scenario prospects whether you are running a business, driving a division, pastoring a congregation, instructing a group, or arranging your individual budgets.

Your objective isn't to be negative or to anticipate the most exceedingly terrible, just to be prepared for it on the off chance that it works out. Like that, you allow yourself the best opportunity for a positive outcome — regardless.

In the event that you picture the most pessimistic scenario and look at it genuinely, you truly have encountered a rude awakening. You're geared up for whatever might happen. As you do that, take the exhortation of Charles Opening, who prompted, "Intentional with alert, however act with choice; and yield with generosity or go against with solidness."

5. Adjust Your Reasoning to Your Assets

One of the keys to augmenting practical reasoning is adjusting your assets to your targets. Taking a gander at upsides and downsides and looking at most pessimistic scenario situations will make you mindful of any holes between what you want and what truly is. When you understand what those holes are, you can utilize your assets to fill them. All things considered, that is the thing assets are for.

SUPER BOWL, SUPER Vault, SUPER SECURITY

Our nation got illustrations in practical reasoning following the awfulness of September 11, 2001. The obliteration of the World Exchange Place structures New York City far outperformed any most pessimistic scenario situations that anybody could have imagined. Directly following that occasion, we currently find that we don't have the advantage of keeping away from or ignoring practical reasoning.

I was helped to remember that on Sunday, February 3, 2002, when I went to the Super Bowl in New Orleans,

Louisiana. I had been to the major event two times previously, to pull for the host group — first San Diego and later Atlanta — and had seen the two groups lose! However, I had never been to a game like this. The event had been assigned a

Public safety Exceptional Occasion. That implied that the U.S. Secret Assistance would regulate it; military faculty would work with neighborhood policing; security would be of the greatest type. The Secret Assistance acquired a few hundred specialists and got the region. In anticipation of the game, admittance to the Super Arch was profoundly confined, with strengthened screening. Authorities closed goes 4x4 romping, shut the close by highway, and assigned the region a restricted air space.

We showed up sooner than expected at the arch — authorities proposed fans show up as long as five hours in front of game time — and we promptly saw proof of the prudent steps. Eight-foot walls encompassed the entire region, and substantial obstructions kept unapproved vehicles from drawing near to the structure. We could see sharpshooters situated at different areas, remembering for the top of a few contiguous structures. At the point when we arrived at an entryway, cops and security faculty tapped us down and inspected everybody's possessions. After that they guided us to go through metal locators. Really at that time did they permit us into the arena?

"That is just fine," you might say, "however what might have happened had there been a fear based oppressor assault?" The Mystery Administration took care of that as well, since they had arranged for the worst situation imaginable. Clearing plans had been established, and work force at the Super Vault had been bored to ensure everybody understood what to do in the event of a crisis.

New Orleans city hall leader Marc Morial said the day preceding the Super Bowl, "We need to make an impression on all guests that New Orleans will be the most secure spot in America." If we received the message. We didn't feel even the slightest bit stressed. That happens when pioneers perceive the significance of reasonable reasoning.

Thinking Question

Am I constructing a strong mental establishment on realities so I can think with certainty?

CHAPTER FIVE

USE KEY REASONING

"A great many people invest more energy arranging their mid-year get-away than arranging their lives."

When you hear the words "vital reasoning," what rings a bell? Do dreams of strategies move in your mind? Do you evoke promoting plans, the sort that can turn an organization around? Maybe you mull over worldwide governmental issues. Or on the other hand you review a portion of history's most noteworthy military missions: Hannibal crossing the Alps to shock the Roman armed force, Charlemagne's triumph of Western Europe, or the Partners' D-Day intrusion of Normandy. Maybe, however procedure doesn't need to be confined to military activity — or even to business. Key reasoning can have a beneficial outcome on any everyday issue.

PLAN YOUR LIFE, Experience YOUR Arrangement

I've seen that a great many people attempt to design their lives each day in turn. They awaken, make up their daily agenda, and jump right into it (albeit certain individuals aren't even that key).

Less people plan their lives each week in turn. They survey their schedule for the week, really take a look at their arrangements, survey their objectives, and afterward get to work. They by and large out achieve the greater part of their day to day arranging associates. I attempt to make arranging one stride further.

Toward the start of each and every month, I go through a portion of a day dealing with my schedule for the following forty days. Forty days works for me as opposed to only thirty. Like that, I get a leap on the following month and don't get shocked. I start by evaluating my itinerary and arranging exercises with my loved ones. Then, at that point, I audit what tasks, examples, and different goals I need to achieve during those five to about a month and a half. Then I begin shutting out days and times for thinking, composing, working, meeting with individuals, and so on. I set times to do fun things, like seeing a show, watching a ball game, or playing golf. I likewise put away little blocks of time to make up for the unforeseen. When I'm finished, I can tell you almost all that I'll do, nearly step by step, during the next few weeks. This methodology is one reason I have had the option to achieve a lot.

WHY YOU Ought to Delivery THE Force OF Vital Reasoning

Key reasoning assists me with arranging, to turn out to be more proficient, to augment my assets, and to track down the most immediate way toward accomplishing any goal. The advantages of vital reasoning are various. The following are a couple of the reasons you ought to take on it as one of your reasoning devices:

1. Vital Reasoning Improves on the Troublesome

Vital reasoning is actually just anticipating steroids. Spanish author Miguel de Cervantes said, "The one who is arranged has his fight half battled." Vital reasoning takes complex issues and long- term targets, which can be extremely challenging to address, and separates them into sensible sizes. Anything becomes more straightforward when it has an arrangement!

Key reasoning can likewise assist you with working on the administration of regular day to day existence. I do that by utilizing frameworks, which are just great systems rehashed. I'm notable among ministers and different speakers for my documenting framework. Composing an example or discourse can be troublesome. But since I utilize my framework to document statements, stories, furthermore, articles, when I want something to sort through or represent a point, I basically go to one of my 1,200 records and find a decent piece of material that works. Pretty much any troublesome undertaking can be simplified with key reasoning.

2. Key Reasoning Prompts You to Pose the Right Inquiries

Would you like to separate intricate or troublesome issues?

Then get clarification on pressing issues. Key reasoning powers you through this cycle. Investigate the accompanying inquiries created by my companion Bobb Biehl, the creator of Master planning.

Heading: What would it be a good idea for us to do straightaway? Why?

Association: Who is answerable for what? Who is answerable for whom?

Do we have the ideal individuals perfectly positioned?

Cash: What is our projected pay, cost, net?

Might we at any point manage the cost of it? How might we bear the cost of it?

Following: Would we say we are on track?

By and large Assessment: Would we say we are accomplishing the quality we expect and request of ourselves?

Refinement: How might we be more powerful and more productive (advance toward the ideal)?

These may not be the main inquiries you want to pose to start concocting an essential strategy, however they are unquestionably a decent beginning.

3. Key Reasoning Prompts Customization

General George S. Patton noticed, "Effective commanders make arrangements to fit conditions, however don't attempt to make conditions to fit plans."

All great key scholars are exact in their reasoning. They attempt to match the methodology to the issue, since system is certainly not a one-size-fits-all recommendation. Messy or summed up believing is an adversary of accomplishment. The expectation to tweak in strategic figuring powers an individual to go past dubious thoughts and participate in unambiguous approaches after an undertaking or issue. It hones the brain.

4. Key Reasoning Sets you up Today for a Questionable Tomorrow

Key reasoning is the extension that joins where you are to where you need to be. It provides guidance and credibility today and builds your true capacity for progress tomorrow. It is, as Mary Webb proposes, such as outfitting your fantasies before you ride them.

5. Key Reasoning Decreases the Safety buffer

Any time you speak plainly or go into an absolutely receptive mode, you increment your edge for blunder. It's like a golf player moving forward to a golf ball and hitting it prior to arranging the shot. Skewing a shot by only a couple degrees can send the ball 100 yards askew. Vital reasoning, notwithstanding, extraordinarily diminishes that edge for mistake. It lines up your activities with your targets, similarly as arranging a shot in golf assists you with putting the ball nearer to the pin. The more adjusted you are with your objective, the more the chances that you will be going in the right course.

6. Key Reasoning Gives You Impact with Others

One leader trusted in another: "Our organization has a short reach plan and a long reach plan. Our short reach plan is to remain above water to the point of coming to our long reach plan." That is not really a methodology, yet that is the position where some business chiefs put themselves. There's more than one issue with ignoring vital reasoning in like that. Besides the fact that it neglects to fabricate the business, however it likewise loses the admiration of everybody associated with the business.

The one with the arrangement is the one with the power. It doesn't make any difference in that frame of mind of action you're included.

Representatives need to follow the business chief with a decent strategy. Volunteers need to get the minister together with a decent service plan. Kids need to be with the grown-up who has the thoroughly examined excursion plan. If you practice vital reasoning, others will pay attention to you and they will need to follow you. In the event that you have a place of administration in an association, vital reasoning is fundamental.

Step by step instructions to Deliver THE POWER OF STRATEGIC THINKING

To improve as an essential mastermind ready to figure out and carry out plans that will accomplish the ideal goal, acknowledge the accompanying rules:

1. Separate the Issue

The most vital phase in essential reasoning is to separate an issue into more modest, more sensible parts so you can zero in on them all the more really. How you do it isn't quite as significant as making it happen. You could separate an issue by capability. That is the thing car trend-setter Henry Passage did when he made the mechanical production system, and that is the reason he said, "Nothing is especially hard assuming you partition it into little positions."

How you split down an issue really depends on you, whether it's by capability, plan, obligation, reason, or another strategy. The fact of the matter is that you really want to separate it. Just a single individual in 1,000,000 can shuffle the entire thing in his mind and think decisively to make strong, suitable plans.

2. Inquire as to Why Before How

At the point when the vast majority start utilizing key reasoning to tackle an issue or plan a method for meeting a goal, they frequently tragically move too soon and attempting promptly to sort out some way to achieve it.

Rather than asking how, they ought to initially inquire as to why. Assuming you bounce directly into critical thinking mode, how can you go to know every one of the issues?

Eugene G. According to effortlessness, "A huge number of specialists can configuration spans, compute strains and stresses, and draw up details for machines, however the incredible designer is the one who can determine if the extension or the machine ought to be worked by any means, where it ought to be fabricated, and while." Inquiring as to why assists you with pondering every one of the explanations behind choices. It assists you with opening your brain to conceivable outcomes and open doors. The size of an opportunity frequently decides the degree of assets and exertion that you should contribute. Large open doors consider critical choices. Assuming you leap to how excessively fast, you could miss that.

3. Recognize the Main problems and Goals

William Plume, creator of The Matter of Life, said, "Before it tends to be tackled, an issue should be plainly characterized." Such a large number of individuals hurry to arrangements, and thus they wind up taking care of some unacceptable issue. To stay away from that, pose testing inquiries to uncover the main problems. Challenge your suspicions as a whole. Gather data even after you think you've distinguished the issue. (You might in any case need to act with deficient information, yet you would rather not rush to make a judgment call before you assemble sufficient data to start recognizing the main problem.) Start by asking, what else could be the main problem you ought to likewise eliminate any private plan. More than nearly whatever else, that can cloud your judgment. Finding what is happening and targets is a significant piece of the fight. When the main problems are distinguished, the arrangements are much of the time basic.

4. Audit Your Assets

I previously referenced how important it is to know about your re-sources, yet it bears rehashing. A technique that doesn't consider assets is ill-fated to disappointment. Take a stock. How long do you have? How much cash? What sorts of materials, supplies, or stock do you have? What are your different resources? What liabilities or commitments will become possibly the most important factor? Which individuals in the group can have an effect? You know your own association and calling. Sort out what assets you have available to you.

5. Foster Your Arrangement

How you approach the arranging system relies extraordinarily upon your calling and the size of the test that you're wanting to handle, so suggesting numerous specifics is troublesome. In any case, regardless of how you go about arranging, take this exhortation: begin with the self-evident. At the point when you tackle an issue or plan that way, it brings solidarity also, agreement to the group, since everybody sees those things. Clear components gather mental speed furthermore, start innovativeness and force. The most effective way to make a street to the complex is to expand on the basics.

6. Put the Ideal Nation Perfectly located

It's important that you incorporate your group as a component of your essential reasoning. Before you can execute your arrangement, you should ensure that you have the perfect individuals set up. Indeed, even the best essential reasoning won't help on the off chance that you don't consider individuals part of the situation. See what occurs assuming that you misjudge:

Wrong Individual: Issues rather than Potential

Wrong Spot: Dissatisfaction rather than Satisfaction Wrong Arrangement: Melancholy rather than Development

Everything meets up, notwithstanding, when you set up each of the three components: the ideal individual, the perfect locations, and the well-conceived plan.

7. 2eep Rehashing the Interaction

My companion Olan Hendrix commented, "Vital reasoning is like showering, you need to continue to make it happen." Assuming that you hope to take care of any serious issue once, you're in for dissatisfaction. Seemingly insignificant details can be won effectively through frameworks and individual discipline. In any case, significant issues need major vital reasoning time. What Thane Yost said is truly obvious: "The will to win is useless in the event that you don't have the will to plan." to be a viable key mastermind, then you really want to turn into a ceaseless vital scholar.

As I was dealing with this part, I went over an article in my nearby paper on the festival of the Jewish

Passover and how a huge number of American Jews read the request for administration for their Seder, or Passover feast, from a little booklet created by Maxwell House Espresso. For over seventy years, the espresso organization has delivered the booklet, called a Haggada, and during those years it has dispersed in excess of 40 million duplicates of it.

"I utilized them for my entire life," said Regina Witt, who is in her fifties. So does her mom, who is very nearly ninety. "It's our custom. I figure it would be exceptionally odd not to utilize them." 9

So how did Maxwell House come to supply the booklets? It was the consequence of key reasoning. Eighty years prior, advertising man Joseph Jacobs prompted that the organization could sell espresso during Passover if the item were ensured Legitimate by a rabbi. (Since 192E,

Maxwell House espresso has been ensured Legitimate for Passover.)

And afterward Jacobs recommended that assuming they offered the Haggada booklets, they could increment deals. 10

They've been making the booklets — and selling espresso during Passover — from that point onward. That can happen when you release the force of key reasoning.

Thinking Question

Am I executing well defined plans that provide me guidance for now and increment my true capacity for tomorrow?

CHAPTER SIX

INVESTIGATE PLAUSIBILITY THINKING

"Nothing is so exceptionally humiliating as watching somebody accomplish something that you said wasn't possible."

Individuals who embrace probability believing are fit for achieving undertakings that appear to be unthinkable on the grounds that they have confidence in arrangements. The following are a few motivations behind why you ought to turn into a chance scholar:

1. Probability Thinking Builds Your Potential outcomes

At the point when you accept you can accomplish something troublesome — and you succeed — numerous entryways open for you. When George Lucas prevailed with regards to making Star Battles, notwithstanding the individuals who said the enhancements he needed hadn't at any point been finished and wasn't possible, numerous different potential outcomes opened dependent upon him. Modern Light and Wizardry (ILM), the organization he made to deliver those "unthinkable" embellishments, turned into a wellspring of income to assist with endorsing his different undertakings. He had the option to create marketing connections to his motion pictures, accordingly acquiring another income stream to subsidize his film making. Be that as it may, his trust in doing the troublesome has likewise made a gigantic effect on other film creators and a totally different age of film participants. Mainstream society author Chris

Deal wicz states, "At first straightforwardly through his own work and afterward by means of the unmatched impact of ILM, George

Lucas has directed for quite a long time the fundamental expansive idea of what is film." 11 On the off chance that you free yourself up to plausibility thinking, you free yourself up to numerous different conceivable outcomes.

2. Probability Thinking Attracts Open doors and Individuals to You

The instance of George Lucas assists you with perceiving how being plausible mastermind can set out new open doors and draw in individuals. Individuals who dream huge draw in enormous individuals to them. If you have any desire to accomplish huge things, you want to turn into a chance mastermind.

3. Plausibility Thinking Builds Others' Prospects

Large scholars who get things going likewise make opportunities for other people. That occurs, to some degree, in light of the fact that it's infectious. You can't resist the urge to turn out to be more certain and dream greater when you're around probability scholars.

4. Probability Thinking Permits you to think ambitiously

Regardless of what you're calling, possibility thinking can assist you with expanding your viewpoints and dream greater dreams. Teacher David J. Schwartz accepts, "Large masterminds are experts in making positive forward-looking, hopeful pictures as far as they could tell and in the personalities of others." On the off chance that you embrace plausibility thinking, your fantasies will go from molehill to mountain size, and in light of the fact that you have confidence in potential outcomes, you set yourself ready to accomplish them.

5. Probability Figuring Makes It Conceivable to Transcend Normal

During the 1970s, when oil costs went through the rooftop, car producers were requested to make their vehicles more eco-friendly. One maker requested a gathering from senior specialists to definitely decrease the heaviness of vehicles they were planning. They took care of on the issue and looked for arrangements, yet they at long last finished up that making lighter vehicles wasn't possible, would be excessively costly, and would introduce such a large number of wellbeing concerns. They couldn't escape the trench of their typical reasoning.

What was the car producer's answer? They gave the issue to a gathering of less-experienced engineers. The new gathering tracked down ways of decreasing the heaviness of the organization's vehicles by many pounds. Since they believed that taking care of the issue was conceivable, it was.

Each time you eliminate the name of unimaginable from an undertaking, you raise your true capacity from normal to out of this world.

6. Plausibility Thinking Gives You Energy

An immediate relationship exists between plausibility thinking and the level of an individual's energy. Who gets stimulated by the possibility of losing? On the off chance that you realize something will fail, how long and energy would you say you will give it? No one goes searching for a waste of time. You put yourself in what you accept can succeed. At the point when you embrace plausibility thinking, you have confidence in the thing you're doing, and that gives you energy.

7. Probability Thinking Holds you back from Surrendering

Most importantly, plausibility scholars accept they can succeed. Denis Waitley, creator of The Brain science of Winning, says, "The victors in life figure continually as far as 'I can, I will and I'm.' Washouts, then again, focus their waking contemplations on what they ought to have done, or what they don't do." On the off chance that you accept you can't follow through with something, then it doesn't make any difference how enthusiastically you attempt, since you've proactively lost. Assuming you accept you can follow through with something, you have proactively won a large part of the fight.

One individuals who demonstrated that he is an extraordinary chance mastermind in 2001 was New York city hall leader Rudy Giuliani. Soon after the World Exchange Community misfortune, Giuliani not just driven the city through the turmoil of the fiasco, however he imparted trust in everybody he contacted. Subsequently, he gave some knowledge and viewpoint on his experience:

I was so pleased with individuals I saw in the city. No tumult, however they were scared and confounded, and I couldn't help suspecting that they expected to hear from my heart where I thought we were going. I was attempting to think, where could I at any point go for a correlation with this, a few examples about how to deal with it? So I began pondering Churchill, began feeling that we must remake the soul of the city, and what preferable model over Churchill and individuals of London during the Barrage in 1940, who needed to keep up their soul during this supported besieging? It was a soothing thought. 12 Sixteen hours after the planes struck the structures in New York City, when Giuliani at last returned at 2:30 A.M. to his loft for a rest, rather than dozing, he read The Second Great War parts of Churchill: A biography by Roy Jenkins. He figured out how Winston Churchill assisted his kin with seeing the conceivable outcomes and made a big difference for his kin. Propelled, Giuliani did likewise for his own kin sixty years after the fact.

The most effective method to FEEL THE ENERGY OFPOSSIBILITY THINKING

On the off chance that you are a normally certain individual who as of now embraces plausibility thinking, you're as of now following me. In any case, certain individuals, as opposed to being hopeful, are normally negative or critical. They accept that chance scholars are innocent or absurd. On the off chance that your reasoning runs toward cynicism, let me pose you an inquiry: what number of exceptionally effective individuals do you have at least some idea who are constantly negative? What number of difficulty masterminds would you say you are familiar with who accomplish enormous things? None! Individuals with an it-isn't possible mentality have two options. They can anticipate the most exceedingly terrible and consistently experience it; or they can transform their mindset. George Lucas did that. In all honesty, despite the fact that he is plausible scholar, he is certainly not a normally sure individual. According to be, "I'm extremely negative, and thus, I think the protection I have against it is to be hopeful. "At the end of the day, he decides to emphatically think. He summarizes it this way: "As silly as it sounds, the force of positive reasoning goes quite far. So assurance and positive thinking joined with ability joined with knowing your specialty… that might seem like an innocent perspective, yet

It's worked for myself as well as it's worked for every one of my companions — so I have come to trust it." 14

On the off chance that you need plausibility remembering to work for you, start by following these ideas:

1. Quit Zeroing in on the Difficulties

The most important phase in turning into a chance scholar is to prevent yourself from looking for and harping on what's amiss with some random circumstance. Sports clinician Sway Rotella describes, "I tell individuals: If you would rather not get into positive reasoning that is not a problem. Simply kill every one of the negative contemplations from your psyche, and anything that's left will be fine."

On the off chance that chance reasoning is unfamiliar to you, you must provide yourself with a great deal of training to dispose of a portion of the negative self-talk you might hear in your mind. At the point when you consequently begin posting everything that can turn out badly or every one of the reasons something isn't possible, stop yourself and say, "Don't go there." Then, at that point, inquire, "Common decency about this?" That will assist with kicking you off. What's more, on the off chance that cynicism is a huge issue for yourself and skeptical things emerge from your mouth before you've even thoroughly examined, you might have to enroll the guide of a companion or relative to caution you each time you utter negative thoughts.

2. Avoid the "Specialists"

Purported specialists accomplish other things to kill individuals' fantasies than pretty much any other individual.

Probability scholars are extremely hesitant to excuse anything as inconceivable. Rocket pioneer Wernher von Braun said, "I have figured out how to utilize the word unimaginable with the best of mindfulness." And Napoleon Bonaparte pronounced, "The word unthinkable isn't in my word reference." Assuming you believe you should accept the guidance of a specialist, notwithstanding, then regard the expressions of John Andrew Holmes, who declared, "Never let a youngster know that something isn't possible. God might have been hanging tight hundreds of years for someone uninformed enough of the difficult to do that thing." If you need to accomplish something, allow yourself to accept it is conceivable — regardless of what specialists could say.

3. Search for Conceivable outcomes in Each Circumstance

Turning into a chance scholar is something other than declining to allow yourself to be negative. It's another component. It's searching for positive prospects notwithstanding the conditions. I as of late heard Wear Soderquist, previous president of Wal-Shop, recount to a great story that represents how an individual can track down certain conceivable outcomes in any circumstance. Soderquist had gone with Sam Walton to Huntsville, Alabama, to open a few new stores. While there, Walton recommended they visit the opposition. This is the very thing Soderquist said occurred: 15

We went into one [store], and I need to let you know that it was the most awful store I've at any point found in my life. It was horrible. There were no clients. There was no assistance on the floor. The paths were jumbled with stock, void racks, messy, it was totally horrible. He [Walton] strolled one way and I'd walk the alternate way and we'd sort of meet out on the walkway. He said, "What'd you think, wear?"

I said, "Sam that is the totally most terrible store I've at any point found in my life. Well, did you see the paths?"

He said, "Wear, did you see the pantyhose rack?"

I said, "No, I didn't, Sam. I probably gone on an unexpected walkway in comparison to you. I didn't see that."

He said, "That was the best pantyhose rack I've at any point seen, Wear." And he said, "I pulled the apparatus out and on the back was the name of the producer. At the point when we get back, I believe you should call that maker and have him come in and visit with our apparatus individuals. I need to place that rack in our stores.

It's totally the best I've at any point seen." And he said straightaway, "Did you see the ethnic beauty care products?"

I said, "Sam that probably been right close to the pantyhose rack, since I totally missed that."

He said, "Wear, do you understand that in our stores we have four feet of ethnic beauty care products. These individuals had 12 feet of it. We are totally passing up this amazing opportunity. I recorded the wholesaler of a portion of those items. At the point when we get back, I believe that you should snag our corrective purchaser and get these individuals in. We totally need to grow our ethnic beauty care products."

Presently, Sam Walton didn't hit me on the head and say, "Wear, presently what illustration did you gain from this?" He had proactively hit me on the head by searching for a long term benefit, looking how to improve, taking a stab at greatness. It's so natural to proceed to take a gander at what others do seriously. Yet, one of the administration qualities of vision that he showed me, and I will always remember it, is search for the positive qualities in the thing others are doing and apply it. It doesn't take a virtuoso intelligence level or twenty years of involvement to track down the chance in each circumstance. Everything necessary is the right demeanor, and anyone can develop that.

4. Dream One Size Greater

One of the most outstanding ways of developing a chance mentality is to incite yourself to dream one size greater than you typically do. Can we just be look at things objectively for a minute: the vast majority dream excessively little? They don't imagine something sufficiently amazing. Henry Curtis prompts, "Make your arrangements as awesome as you like, since a quarter century from now, they will appear to be unremarkable. Make your arrangements multiple times according to plan, and a quarter century from now you will ask why you didn't make them multiple times as perfect."

In the event that you drive yourself to dream all the more expansively, to envision your association one size greater, to make your objectives basically a stage past what makes you agreeable, you will be compelled to develop. What's more, it will get you in a position to trust in bigger potentials.

5. 6uestion the Status 6uo

The vast majority believe their lives should continue to improve, yet they esteem harmony and dependability simultaneously. Individuals frequently fail to remember that you can't improve yet remain something similar. Development implies change. Change requires rocking the boat. In the event that you need bigger potentials, you can't make do with what you have now. At the point when you become a chance scholar, you will confront many individuals who will maintain that you should surrender your fantasies and embrace business as usual. Achievers will not acknowledge the state of affairs.

As you investigate more amazing things for yourself, your association, or your family — and others challenge you for it — breathe easy in light of realizing that right now as you read this, other chance masterminds across the nation and all over the planet are contemplating restoring malignant growth, growing new energy sources, taking care of hungry individuals, and working on personal satisfaction. They are rocking the boat despite everything — and you ought to, as well.

6. Track down Motivation from Incredible Achievers

You can gain some significant knowledge about plausibility thinking by concentrating on incredible achievers. I referenced George Lucas in this part. Maybe he doesn't interest you, or you could do without the film business. (By and by, I'm not a major sci-fi fan, however I respect Lucas as a mastermind, imaginative visionary, and money manager.) Kind some achievers you respect and study them. Search for individuals with the disposition of Robert K. Kennedy, who advocated George Bernard Shaw's mixing articulation: "A few men see things as they are and say, 'Why?' I long for things that never were and say, 'What difference would it make?'"

I realize probability believing isn't in style with many individuals. So call it what you like: the will to succeed, faith in yourself, trust in your capacity, confidence. It's truly obvious: individuals who accept they can't, don't. Yet, in the event that you accept you can, you can! That is the force of probability thinking.

Thinking Question

Am I releasing the excitement of plausibility remembering to find answers for even apparently unthinkable situations*

CHAPTER SEVEN

GAIN FROM INTELLIGENT REASONING

"To uncertainty everything or to accept everything are two similarly helpful arrangements; both shed the need of reflection."

The speed of our general public doesn't energize intelligent reasoning. A great many people would prefer to act than think. Presently, try not to misunderstand me. I'm an individual of activity. I have exceptionally high energy and I like to see things achieved. In any case

I'm likewise an intelligent scholar. Intelligent reasoning resembles the Simmering pot of the psyche. It urges your contemplations to stew until they're finished. As I go through this cycle, I want to reflect so I could gain from my triumphs and errors, find what I ought to attempt to rehash, and figure out what I ought to change. It is consistently a significant activity. By intellectually visiting past circumstances, you can think with more prominent comprehension.

1. Intelligent Reasoning Gives You Genuine Viewpoint

At the point when our kids were youthful nevertheless inhabited home, we used to take them on superb excursions each year. At the point when we returned home, they generally realize that I planned to pose them two inquiries: "What did you like best?" and "What did you realize?" It didn't make any difference whether we went to Walt Disney World or Washington, D.C.

I generally posed those inquiries. Why? Since I believed that they should think about their encounters. Youngsters try not to normally get a handle on the worth (or cost) of an experience except if incited. They underestimate things. I believed that my kids should see the value in our outings and to gain from them. At the point when you reflect, you can put an experience into point of view. You can assess its timing. What's more, you can acquire another appreciation for things that before slipped through the cracks. The vast majority can perceive the penances of their folks or other individuals just when they become guardians themselves. That is the sort of viewpoint that accompanies reflection.

2. Intelligent Reasoning Gives Profound Honesty to Your Thought Life

Hardly any individuals have great point of view in the intensity of a close to home second. Most people who partake in the rush of an encounter attempt to return and recover it without first attempting to assess it. (It's one reason our way of life creates so many daredevils.) In like manner, the people who endure a horrible encounter normally keep away from comparative circumstances no matter what, which now and again integrates them with close to home bunches.

Intelligent reasoning empowers you to move away from the extraordinary feelings of especially positive or negative encounters and see them with an open-minded perspective. You can see the adventures of the past in the illumination of profound development and look at misfortunes in the radiance of truth and rationale. That interaction can assist an individual with halting hauling around a lot of pessimistic psychological weight.

President George Washington noticed, "We should not to think back except if it is to determine valuable illustrations from past mistakes, and for the motivation behind benefitting by beyond all doubt purchased insight." Any inclination that can bear upping to the radiance of truth and can be supported over the long haul has close to home trustworthiness and is consequently deserving of your psyche and heart.

3. Intelligent Reasoning Expands Your Trust in Direction

Have you made a snap judgment and later contemplated whether you made the best choice? Everyone has.

Intelligent reasoning can assist with diffusing that uncertainty. It additionally gives you certainty for the following choice. Whenever you've thought about an issue, you don't need to rehash each step of the reasoning system when you're confronted with it once more. You have mental street markers from having been there previously. That packs and rates up thinking time — and it gives you certainty. Furthermore, over the long run, it can likewise fortify your instinct.

4. Intelligent Reasoning Explains the Higher perspective

At the point when you participate in intelligent reasoning, you can place thoughts and encounters into a more precise setting.

Intelligent reasoning urges us to return and invest energy considering what we have done and what we have seen. In the event that an individual who loses his employment considers what occurred, he might see an example of occasions that prompted his excusal. He will better comprehend what occurred, why it worked out, and what things were his obligation. If he likewise takes a gander at the occurrences that happened a while later, he might understand that at the end of the day, lucky to be in his new position since it better accommodates his abilities and wants. Without reflection, it tends to be extremely challenging to understand the situation completely.

5. Intelligent Reasoning Takes a Decent Encounter and Makes It a Significant Encounter

At the point when you were simply beginning in your profession, did it appear to be that couple of individuals were able to give somebody without experience an open door? Simultaneously, might you at any point see individuals who had been on their positions twenty years who at this point took care of their responsibilities inadequately? Assuming this is the case that most likely baffled you. Writer William Shakespeare expressed, "Experience is a gem, and it had need be thus, for it is frequently bought at a limitless rate." Yet, experience alone doesn't increase the value of a daily existence. It's not be guaranteed to encounter that is important; it's the knowledge individuals gain due to their experience. Intelligent reasoning transforms insight into knowledge.

Mark Twain said, "We ought to be mindful so as to escape an encounter all the insight that is in it dislike the feline that plunks down on a hot oven top. She won't ever plunk down on a hot oven top from now on — and that is well; yet in addition she won't ever plunk down on a cool one any longer." 16 An encounter becomes important when it illuminates or prepares us to meet new encounters. Intelligent reasoning assists with doing that.

The most effective method to EMBRACE THE Examples OF Intelligent Reasoning

Assuming that you resemble a great many people in our way of life today, you most likely do next to no intelligent reasoning. Assuming that is the case, it very well might be keeping you down more than you suspect. Acknowledge the accompanying ideas to build your capacity to brilliantly think:

1. Put away Opportunity for Reflection

Greek scholar Socrates noticed, "The unexamined life does not merit living." For the vast majority, be that as it may, reflection and self-assessment doesn't work out easily. It tends to be a genuinely awkward movement for an assortment of reasons: they struggle with keeping on track; they find the interaction dull; or they could do without spending a great deal of time pondering sincerely troublesome issues. Yet, on the off chance that you don't cut out the ideal opportunity for it, you are probably not going to do any intelligent reasoning.

2. Eliminate Yourself from Interruptions

However much some other thought process, reflection requires isolation. Interruption and reflection basically don't blend. It's not the sort of thing you can do well approach a TV, in a work space, while the telephone is ringing, or with kids in a similar room.

One reason I've had the option to achieve a lot and continue to develop by and by is that I've made opportunity to reflect, yet I've isolated myself from interruptions for short blocks of time: thirty minutes in the spa; an hour outside on a stone in my patio; or a couple of hours in an agreeable seat in my office. The spot doesn't make any difference — as long as you eliminate yourself from interruptions and interferences.

3. Routinely Survey Your Schedule or Diary

A great many people utilize their schedule as an arranging instrument, which it is. However, not many individuals use it as an intelligent reasoning device. What could be better, notwithstanding, for assisting you with exploring where you have been and what you have done

—but perhaps a diary? I'm not a journal in the ordinary sense; I don't utilize writing to sort out what I'm thinking and feeling. All things being equal, I sort out the thing I'm thinking and believing, and afterward I record huge considerations and activity focuses. (I record the contemplations so I can immediately put my hands on them once more. I promptly execute the activity focuses or delegate them to another person.)

Schedules and diaries help you to remember how you've invested your energy, show you whether your exercises match your needs, and assist you with seeing whether you are gaining ground. They additionally offer you a valuable chance to review exercises that you probably won't had opportunity and willpower to ponder already. The absolute most significant contemplations you've at any point had may have been lost since you didn't give yourself the reflection time you wanted.

4. Ask the Right 0uestions

The worth you get from considering will depend the sorts of inquiries you pose to yourself. The better the inquiries, the more gold you will mine from your reasoning. At the point when I reflect, I think concerning my qualities, connections, and encounters. Here are some example questions:

Self-awareness: What have I realized today that will assist me with developing? How might I apply it to my life? When would it be a good idea for me to apply it?

Adding Worth: To whom did I add esteem today? How would I realize I enhanced that individual? Might I at any point follow up and intensify the positive advantage the person got?

Authority: Did I show others how it's done today? Did I lift my kin and association to a more significant level? How did I respond and how could I make it happen?

Individual Confidence: Did I address God well today? Did I rehearse the Brilliant Rule? Have I "strolled the subsequent mile" with somebody?

Marriage and Family: Did I convey love to my family today? How could I show that adoration? Did they feel it? Did they bring it back?

Inward Circle: Have I invested sufficient energy with my vital participants? How might I assist them with finding lasting success? In what regions could I at any point guide them?

Revelations: What was it that I experience today to which I want to give seriously thinking time? Are there examples to be learned? Are there action items?

How you sort out your appearance time depends on you. You might need to adjust my example to your own qualities. Or on the other hand you can attempt a framework that my companion Dick Biggs utilizes. He makes three sections on a piece of paper:

Year defining moment Effect

This framework is great for pondering the master plan. Dick utilized it to see designs in his day to day existence, for example, when he moved to Atlanta and was empowered by another educator to compose. You could straightforwardly express "Occasion,"

"Importance," and "Activity Point" on a page to assist you with profiting from intelligent reasoning. The central thing is to bring up issues that work for you, and record any critical considerations that come to you during the reflection time.

5. Concrete Your Learning through Activity

Recording the great considerations that emerge from your intelligent reasoning has esteem, however nothing assists you with developing like setting your contemplations in motion. That's what to do, you should be purposeful. At the point when you read a decent book, for instance, there are in every case great considerations, statements, or examples that you can detract from it and use yourself. I generally mark the focal points in a book and afterward rehash them when I'm finished with the book. At the point when I stand by listening to a message, I record the important points with the goal that I can document them for some time later. At the point when I go to a course, I take great notes, and I utilize an arrangement of images to prompt me to do specific things:

A bolt like this → means to take a gander at this material once more.

A reference bullet like this * close to an obvious segment means to document it as indicated by the subject noted.

A section like this [implies that I need to utilize what's undeniable in a talk or book. A bolt like this C method this thought will take off assuming I work at it.

At the point when a great many people go to a gathering or course, they partake in the experience, pay attention to the speakers, and now and again even take notes. Be that as it may, nothing occurs after they return home. They like a considerable lot of the ideas they hear, yet when they close their note pads, they don't reconsider them. At the point when that occurs, they get minimal in excess of a transitory flood of inspiration. At the point when you go to a meeting, return to what you heard, consider it, and afterward set it in motion; it can completely change you.

Eventually, intelligent reasoning has three primary qualities: it gives me point of view inside setting; it permits me to constantly associate with my excursion; and it gives guidance and bearing concerning my future. It is a significant instrument to my self-awareness. Barely any things in life can help me learn and further develop the way intelligent thinking can.

Thinking Question

Am I routinely returning to the past to acquire a genuine point of view and think with understanding?

CHAPTER EIGHT

QUESTION WELL KNOWN THINKING

"I'm not a replying mail, I'm a scrutinizing machine. On the off chance that we have every one of the responses, why we're in such a wreck?"

Business analyst John Maynard Keynes, whose thoughts significantly affected monetary hypothesis and practices in the

20th 100 years, stated, "The trouble lies not such a great amount in growing novel thoughts as in getting away from the old ones." Conflicting with well-known speculation can be troublesome, whether you're a finance manager kicking organization custom, a minister acquainting new kinds of music with his congregation, another mother dismissing old spouses' stories gave over from her folks, or a young person disregarding presently well-known styles.

A large number of the thoughts in this book conflict with famous reasoning. In the event that you esteem prominence over very smart, you will seriously restrict your capability to gain proficiency with the kinds of reasoning empowered by this book.

Well known believing is…

- Excessively Normal to Figure out the Worth of Very savvy,
- Excessively Resolute to Understand the Effect of Changed Thinking,
- Excessively Languid to Dominate the Course of Deliberate Reasoning,
- Excessively Little to See the Insight of Higher perspective Reasoning,
- Excessively Fulfilled to Release the Capability of Centered Thinking,
- Excessively Conventional to Find the Delight of Innovative Reasoning,

Too Credulous to Perceive the Significance of Reasonable Reasoning,

- Excessively Disorderly to Delivery the Force of Vital Reasoning,
- Excessively Restricting to Feel the Energy of Plausibility Thinking,
- Excessively In vogue to Embrace the Illustrations of Intelligent Reasoning,
- Excessively Shallow to Scrutinize the Acknowledgment of Famous Reasoning,
- Excessively Glad to Support the Interest of Shared Thinking,
- Excessively Narcissistic to Experience the Fulfillment of Unselfish Reasoning, and Excessively Uncertain to Partake in the Arrival of Primary concern Thinking.

If you have any desire to turn into a decent mastermind, then begin setting yourself up for the chance of becoming disliked.

WHY YOU Ought to Scrutinize the Acknowledgment OF Famous Reasoning

I've given you a few wide explanations behind scrutinizing the acknowledgment of well-known thinking. Presently permit me to be more unambiguous:

1. Well known Speculation In some cases Means Not Thinking

My companion Kevin Myers summarizes the possibility of well-known speculation by saying, "The issue with famous reasoning is that it doesn't expect you to think by any means." Very savvy is difficult work. In the event that it were simple, everyone would be a decent mastermind. Tragically, many individuals attempt to carry on with life the simple way. They would rather not accomplish the difficult work of reasoning or follow through on the cost of achievement. It's simpler to do what others do and trust that they thought it out.

Check out at the financial exchange proposals of certain specialists. When they distribute their picks, most are pursuing a direction, not making one or in any event, riding its peak. Individuals who will bring in cash on the stocks they suggest have proactively done as such when the overall population catches wind of it. At the point when individuals indiscriminately pursue a direction, they're not doing their own reasoning.

2. Famous Reasoning Offers Bogus Expectation

Benno Muller-Slope, a teacher in the College of Cologne hereditary qualities division, tells how one morning in secondary school he stood toward the end in a line of forty understudies in the schoolyard. His physical science educator had set up a telescope so his understudies could see a planet and its moons. The main understudy moved forward to the telescope. He glanced through it, yet when the educator inquired as to whether he could see anything, the kid said no; his myopia hampered his view. The instructor told him the best way to change the concentration, and the kid at last said he could see the planet and moons.

Individually, the understudies moved forward to the telescope and saw what they should see. At last, the second to last understudy investigated the telescope and reported that he was unable to see anything.

"You nitwit," yelled the instructor, "You need to change the focal points."

The understudy attempted, however he at last said, "I actually can't see anything. It is all dark."

The instructor, sickened, glanced through the telescope himself, and afterward turned upward with an unusual articulation. The focal point cap actually covered the telescope. None of the understudies had the option to see anything! 17

Many individuals search for wellbeing and security in famous reasoning. That's what they figure in the event that a many individuals are following through with something, it should be correct. It should be really smart. On the off chance that the vast majority acknowledge it, it most likely addresses reasonableness, fairness, sympathy, and awareness, correct? Not really. Famous reasoning said the earth was the focal point of the universe, at this point Copernicus concentrated on the stars and planets and demonstrated numerically that the earth and different planets in our planetary group rotated around the sun. Well known speculation said a medical procedure didn't need clean instruments, yet Joseph Lister concentrated on the high passing rates in emergency clinics and presented sterile rehearses that promptly saved lives. Well known speculation said that ladies shouldn't reserve the privilege to cast a ballot, yet individuals like Emmeline Pankhurst and Susan B. Anthony battled for and won that right. Famous reasoning put the Nazis into power in Germany, yet Hitler's system killed millions and almost obliterated Europe. We should continuously bear in mind there is an immense contrast among acknowledgment and knowledge. Individuals might express that there's security in larger groups, yet entirely that is false all the time.

Now and again clearly well-known believing isn't great and right. Different times it's less obvious. For instance, consider the stunning number of individuals in the US who have added to a lot of obligation on their Visas. Any individual who is monetarily keen will let you know that is an ill-conceived notion. However millions follow right alongside the well-known considering purchase presently, pay later. Thus they endlessly pay. Many commitments of Well-known speculation ring empty. Try not to allow them to trick you.

3. Famous Reasoning Is Delayed to Embrace Change

Well known speculation adores the norm. It places its trust in the possibility existing apart from everything else, and clutches it energetically. Accordingly, it opposes change and hoses development. Donald M. Nelson, previous leader of the General public of Autonomous Film Makers, condemned famous reasoning when he attested, "We should dispose of the possibility that previous daily practice, past approaches to getting things done, are presumably the most effective ways. In actuality, we should expect that there is most likely a superior method for doing nearly everything. We should quit expecting that a thing which has never been finished before most likely isn't possible by any means."

4. Well known Speculation Brings Just Normal Outcomes

The primary concern? Famous reasoning brings fair outcomes. Here is famous reasoning basically:

> Famous = Ordinary = Normal

It's the least of the best and the best of the least. We limit our prosperity when we take on famous reasoning. It addresses investing minimal effort to simply squeeze by. You should dismiss normal reasoning if you have any desire to achieve remarkable outcomes.

Instructions to Scrutinize THE Acknowledgment OF Well-known THINKING

Well known speculation has frequently discredited and restricting. Addressing it isn't really hard, when you develop the propensity for doing as such. The trouble is in getting everything rolling. Start by doing the accompanying things:

1. Think Before You Follow

Numerous people follow others consequently. Some of the time they do so on the grounds that they want to follow the easiest course of action. Different times they dread dismissal. Or on the other hand they trust there's astuteness in doing what every other person does. In any case, to succeed, you want to contemplate what's ideal, not what's famous.

Moving well known believing requires a readiness to be disagreeable and go beyond the standard. Following the awfulness of September 11, 2001, for instance, scarcely any individuals energetically decided to go via plane. In any case, that was the best chance to travel: swarms were down, security was up, and carriers were reducing costs. About a month after the misfortune, my better half, Margaret, and I heard that Broadway shows had bunches of seats and numerous New York lodgings stayed void. Famous reasoning said, avoid New York. We involved that as an open door. We got modest boarding passes to the city, booked a room in an extraordinary inn for about marked down, and got passes to the most pursued show: The Makers. As we sat down in the theater, we sat close to a lady next to herself with fervor.

"I can't accept I'm at long last here," she shared with us. "I've stood by so lengthy. This is the best show on Broadway

—what's more, the hardest to get passes to." Then, at that point, she went to look at me without flinching and said, "I've had my tickets for 18 months, standing by to see this show. How quite a while in the past did you get yours?"

"You won't approve of my response," I answered.

"Goodness, come on," she said. "How long?"

"I got mine five days prior," I replied. She checked out at us with sickening apprehension. Coincidentally, she was correct. It's quite possibly of the best show we've found in some time. Also, we got to see it simply because we were ready to conflict with famous reasoning when every other person was remaining at home.

As you naturally suspect contrary to what would be expected of famous reasoning, advise yourself that

Disliked thinking, in any event, while bringing about progress, is to a great extent misjudged, unnoticed, and misconstrued.

Disliked speculation contains the seeds of vision and opportunity. Disliked believing is expected for all advancement.

The following time you feel prepared to adjust to famous reasoning on an issue, pause and think. You probably shouldn't make change for the wellbeing of its own, however you surely don't have any desire to indiscriminately understand in light of the fact that you haven't contemplated what's ideal.

2. Value thinking not the same as Your Own

One of the ways of embracing advancement and change is to figure out how to see the value by the way others think. That's what to do, you should constantly open yourself to individuals not quite the same as yourself. My sibling, Larry Maxwell — a decent money manager and an inventive mastermind — constantly challenges well known speculation by thinking in an unexpected way. He says:

The majority of our kin in deals and center administration come from organizations with items and administrations unique in relation to our own. That continually opens us to better approaches for thinking. We likewise deter our kin from dynamic support in conventional business and exchange affiliations and clubs in light of the fact that their reasoning is very normal. They don't have to invest bunches of energy thinking the way every other person in the business does.

As you endeavor to challenge well known thinking, invest energy with individuals with various foundations, training levels, proficient encounters, individual interests, and so forth. You will think like individuals with whom you invest the most energy. Assuming you invest energy with individuals who consider out the crate, you're bound to challenge well known thinking and kick off something new.

3. Ceaselessly Question Your Own Reasoning

Can we just be real for a moment, any time we track down a perspective that works, one of our most noteworthy enticements is to return to it over and over, regardless of whether it no longer functions admirably. The best foe to-morrow's prosperity is some of the time the present victory.

My companion Andy Stanley as of late shown an initiative illustration at INJOY's Impetus Gathering called "Testing the Interaction." He portrayed how progress should be gone before by change, and he brought up quite a large number of the elements associated with addressing famous reasoning. In an association, he said, we ought to recollect that each custom was initially smart — and maybe even progressive. In any case, each custom may not be a smart thought for what's in store.

In your association, on the off chance that you were engaged with establishing what presently exists, almost certainly, you will oppose improve — even change. That is the reason testing your own thinking is significant. In the event that you're excessively joined to your own reasoning and how everything is done now, then nothing will improve.

4. Attempt New Things in New Ways

When did you last work on something interestingly? Do you abstain from facing challenges or attempting new things?

One of the most incredible ways of escaping the trench of your own reasoning is to develop. You can do that in little, regular ways: drive to work an alternate way from ordinary. Request a new dish at your number one café. Ask a different partner to assist you with a natural venture. Remove yourself from autopilot.

Disliked speculation clarifies some things and looks for choices. In 1997, my three organizations moved to Atlanta, Georgia. It's an extraordinary city, however traffic at busy times can get insane. Following moving here, I started looking for and testing elective courses to wanted objections with the goal that I wouldn't be trapped in rush hour gridlock. From my home to the air terminal, for instance, I have found and utilized nine courses inside eight miles and a short ways from each other. Frequently I'm astonished to see individuals sitting on the road when they could be pushing ahead on an elective course. The issue lies with what? An excessive number of individuals have not attempted new things in new ways. It is valid: most individuals are happier with old issues than focused on tracking down new arrangements.

How you approach doing new things in new ways isn't generally as significant as ensuring you make it happen. (Plus, assuming you attempt to do new things similarly that every other person does, would you say you are truly conflicting with well-known thinking? H Get out there and accomplish something else today.

5. Get Use1 to Being Awkward

All things considered, well known believing is agreeable. It resembles an old chair changed in accordance with every one of the proprietor's quirks. The issue with most old chairs is that nobody has loo end at them recently. Assuming this is the case, they'd concur that now is the ideal time to get another one! To dismiss famous reasoning to embrace accomplishment, you'll need to become accustomed to being awkward.

On the off chance that you embrace disliked thinking and settle on choices in light of what works best and what is correct as opposed to what is generally acknowledged, know this: in your initial years you will not be all around as off-base as individuals suspect you are. In your later years, you will not be basically as right as individual suspect you are. And all as the years progressed, you will be better than you naturally suspected you could be.

Thinking Question

Am I deliberately dismissing the limits of normal reasoning to achieve unprecedented results?

CHAPTER NINE

BENEFIT FROM SHARED THINKING

"Not a single one of us is basically as shrewd as us all."

Great scholars, particularly the individuals who are likewise great pioneers, grasp the force of shared thinking. They know that when they esteem the contemplations and thoughts of others, they get the intensifying aftereffects of shared thinking and achieve more than they at any point could all alone.

The people who partake in shared speculation figure out the accompanying:

1. Shared Believing Is Quicker than Solo Reasoning

We live in a genuinely quick moving world. To work at its ongoing pace, we can't go solo. I think the age of young fellows and ladies simply entering the labor force sense that unequivocally.

Maybe to that end they esteem local area so profoundly and are bound to work for an organization they like than one that compensates them fairly. Working with others resembles giving yourself an easy route.

To get familiar with another ability rapidly, how would you make it happen? Do you go off without anyone else and sort it out, or do you get somebody to show you how? You can constantly advance all the more rapidly from somebody with experience — whether you're attempting to figure out how to utilize another product bundle, foster your golf swing, or cook another dish.

2. Shared Believing Is More Creative than Solo Reasoning

We will generally consider extraordinary masterminds and trailblazers soloists, however in all actuality the best imaginative thinking doesn't happen in a vacuum. Advancement results from coordinated effort. Albert Einstein once commented, "Frequently I understand how much my own external and internal life is based upon the works of my kindred men, both living and dead, and how sincerely I should endeavor to offer as a tradeoff however much I have gotten."

Shared speculation prompts more noteworthy advancement, whether you take a gander at crafted by specialists Marie and Pierre Curie, surrealists Luis Brunel and Salvador Dali, or lyricists John Lennon and Paul McCartney. In the event that you consolidate your considerations with the contemplations of others, you won't think of considerations you've ever had!

3. Shared Speculation Brings More Development than Solo Reasoning

However much we might want to imagine that we know everything, every one of us is presumably horrendously mindful of our visually impaired spots and areas of freshness. At the point when I initially began as a minister, I had dreams and energy, yet little experience. To attempt to conquer that, I endeavored to get a few high-profile ministers of developing chapels to impart their reasoning to me. In the mid-1970s, I composed letters to the ten best ministers in the nation, offering them what was an enormous measure of cash to me at that point ($100) to meet me for 60 minutes, so I could ask them inquiries. At the point when one said OK, I'd visit him. I didn't talk a lot, but to pose a couple of inquiries. I wasn't there to intrigue anybody or fulfill my inner self. I was there to learn. I paid attention to all that he said, took cautious notes, and assimilated all that I could. Those encounters completely changed me.

You've had encounters I haven't, and I've had encounters you haven't. Set up us and we bring a more extensive scope of individual history — and subsequently development — to the table. On the off chance that you don't have the experience you want, attach with somebody who does.

4. Shared Believing is more grounded than Solo Reasoning

Scholar writer Johann Wolfgang von Goethe said, "To acknowledge solid counsel is however to build one's own capacity." Two heads are superior to one — when they are thinking in a similar course. It resembles tackling two ponies to pull a cart. They are more grounded arranging than either is exclusively. However, did you had at least some idea that when they arrange, they can move more weight than the amount of what they can move independently? A cooperative energy comes from cooperating. That equivalent sort of energy becomes possibly the most important factor when individuals think together.

5. Shared Speculation Returns more prominent Worth than Solo Reasoning

Since shared believing is more grounded than solo reasoning, clearly it yields a better yield. That happens in view of the intensifying activity of shared thinking. However, it additionally offers different advantages. The individual return you get from shared thinking and encounters can be perfect. Clarence Francis summarizes the advantages in the accompanying perception: "I earnestly accept that the word connections is the way in to the possibility of a nice world. It appears to be completely clear that each issue you will have — in your family, in your work, in our country, or in this world — is basically a question of connections, of relationship."

6. Shared Believing Is the Best way to Have Extraordinary Reasoning

I accept that each extraordinary thought starts with three or four smart thoughts. What's more, most smart thoughts come from shared thinking. Writer Ben Jonson said, "He that is educated exclusively without help from anyone else has a blockhead for an expert."

At the point when I was in school, educators put the accentuation on being correct and on showing improvement over different understudies, seldom on cooperating to think of smart responses. However every one of the responses improve when they utilize everybody's reasoning. On the off chance that we each have one thought, and together we have two contemplations, we generally have the potential for an extraordinary idea.

Step by step instructions to Support THE Investment OF SHARED THINKING

Certain individuals normally take part in shared thinking. Any time they see an issue, they think, who do I have at least some idea who can assist with this? Pioneers will more often than not be like that. Extroverts do as well. Notwithstanding, you don't need to be both of those to profit from shared thinking. As the accompanying moves toward assist you with working on your capacity to bridle shared thinking:

1. Esteem the Thoughts of Others

To start with, accept that the thoughts of others have esteem. In the event that you don't, your options will be limited. How can you say whether you really need input from others? Pose yourself these inquiries:

Am I genuinely secure? Individuals who need certainty and stress over their status, position, or power will generally dismiss the thoughts of others, safeguard their turf, and keep individuals under control. It takes a protected individual to think about others' thoughts. Quite a while back, a genuinely uncertain individual took a vital situation on my leading group of chiefs. After two or three gatherings, it ended up being clear to the next board individuals that this person wouldn't decidedly add to the association. I asked a carefully prepared pioneer on the board, "For what reason does this individual generally do and make statements that upset our advancement?" I will always remember his answer: "Harming individuals hurt individuals."

Do I put esteem on individuals? You won't esteem the thoughts of an individual in the event that you don't esteem and regard the individual oneself. Have you at any point viewed as you're direct around individuals you esteem, versus those you don't? Check the distinctions out:

Do I esteem the intelligent process? A magnificent collaboration frequently happens as the aftereffect of shared thinking.

It can take you puts you've won't ever be. Distributer Malcolm Forbes declared, "Paying attention to counsel frequently achieves definitely more than regarding it." I should say, I didn't necessarily esteem shared thinking. For numerous years, I would in general pull out when I needed to foster thoughts. Just hesitantly accomplished I work on thoughts with others. At the point when a partner tested me on this, I began to dissect my reluctance. That's what I understood it returned to my school insight. Occasionally in the study hall I could perceive that an educator was ill-equipped to address and on second thought invested the class energy requesting that we offer our clueless perspectives on a subject. More often than not, the feelings appeared to be no greater than mine. I had come to class so that the teacher could educate me. I understood that the most common way of sharing thoughts wasn't the issue; it was who was communicating everything. Shared believing is just all around as great as individuals doing the sharing. Since learning that example, I have embraced the intuitive cycle, and presently I accept it is one of my assets. In any case, I continuously contemplate whom I bring around the table for a common reasoning meeting. (I'll tell you my rules for whom I welcome later in this section.)

You should free yourself up to sharing thoughts before you will take part during the time spent shared thinking.

2. Move from Rivalry to Participation

Jeffrey J. Fox, creator of How to Become Chief, says, "Forever be keeping watch for thoughts. Be totally unpredictable regarding the source. Get thoughts from clients, kids, contenders, different ventures, or taxi drivers. It doesn't make any difference who came up with something." 18

An individual who values collaboration wants to finish the thoughts of others, not rival them. If somebody requests that you share thoughts, center around aiding the group, not excelling by and by. Furthermore, in the event that you are the person who unites individuals to share their considerations, acclaim the thought more than the wellspring of the thought. Assuming the smartest thought generally wins (instead of the individual who offered it), then all will impart their considerations to more noteworthy excitement.

3. Have a Plan When You Meet

I appreciate investing energy with specific individuals, regardless of whether we talk about thoughts: my better half, Margaret; my kids; my grandkids; my folks. However we frequently talk about thoughts, it doesn't annoy me on the off chance that we don't; we are family. At the point when I invest energy with almost any other person in my life, nonetheless, I have a plan. I understand what I need to achieve.

The more I regard the insight of the individual, the more I tune in. For instance, when I meet with somebody I'm coaching, I let the individual pose the inquiries, however I hope to do the majority of the talking. At the point when I meet with somebody who guides me, I generally keep my mouth shut. In different connections, the compromise is all the more even. However, regardless of with whom I meet, I have a justification for getting together and I have an assumption for what I'll provide for it and get from it. That is valid whether it's for business or joy.

4. Get the Perfect Nation around the Table

To get anything of significant worth out of shared thinking, you want to have individuals around who offer something that would be useful. As you get ready to request that individuals take part in shared thinking, utilize the accompanying measures for the choice cycle. Pick:

- Individuals who's most noteworthy longing is the outcome of the thoughts.
- Individuals who can enhance another's considerations.
- Individuals who can genuinely deal with fast changes in the discussion.

- Individuals who value the qualities of others in regions where they are feeble.
- Individuals who figure out their place of significant worth at the table.
- Individuals who place what is best for the group before themselves.
- Individuals who can draw out the best reasoning in individuals around them.
- Individuals who have development, experience, and progress in the issue being talked about. Individuals who will assume a sense of ownership with choices.
- Individuals who will leave the table with a "we" demeanor, not a "me" disposition.

Time and again we pick our conceptualizing accomplices in light of sensations of kinship or conditions or accommodation. However, that doesn't assist us with finding and make the thoughts of the greatest request. Who we welcome to the table has a significant effect.

5. Remunerate Great Masterminds and Associates Well

Fruitful associations practice shared thinking. On the off chance that you lead an association, division, or group, then you can't stand to be without individuals who are great at shared thinking. As you select and recruit, search for good masterminds who esteem others, have insight with the cooperative interaction, and are sincerely secure. Then, at that point, compensate them fairly and challenge them to utilize their reasoning abilities and offer their thoughts frequently. Nothing adds esteem like a ton of good masterminds assembling their brains.

Regardless of what you're attempting to achieve, you can improve shared thinking. For that reason I go through quite a bit of my time on earth educating authority. Great administration assists with assembling the perfect individuals brilliantly for the right reason so everyone wins. Everything necessary is the perfect individuals and a readiness to take part in shared thinking.

Thinking Question

Am I reliably including the heads of others to think "over my head" and accomplish compounding results?

CHAPTER TEN

PRACTICE UNSELFISH REASONING

"We can't hold a light to light one more's way without lighting up our own."

Such a long ways in this book, we've examined numerous perspectives that can assist you with accomplishing more. Every one of them can possibly make you more effective. Presently I need to familiarize you with a thought process with the potential to transform yourself in another manner. It could try and reclassify how you view achievement.

Unselfish reasoning can frequently convey a return more prominent than some other perspective. Investigate a portion of its advantages:

1. Unselfish Reasoning Brings Individual Satisfaction

Scarcely any things in life bring more noteworthy individual awards than helping other people.

Charles H. Burr accepted, "Getters for the most part don't get bliss; providers get it." Aiding individuals brings extraordinary fulfillment. At the point when you go through your day unselfishly serving others, around evening time you can set out your head without any second thoughts and rest sufficiently. In

Drawing out the Best in Individuals, Alan Loy McGinnis commented, "There is not any more honorable occupation in that frame of mind than to help another person — to assist somebody with succeeding."

Regardless of whether you have gone through quite a bit of your time on earth chasing after egotistical increase, having a shift in perspective is rarely past the point of no return. Indeed, even the most hopeless individual, similar to Charles Dickens' Miser, can turn his life around and make a distinction for other people. Alfred Nobel did that. At the point when he saw his own eulogy in the paper (his sibling had passed on and the manager had expounded on some unacceptable Nobel, saying that the explosives his organization delivered had killed many individuals), Nobel promised to advance harmony and recognize commitments to humankind. That is the manner by which the Nobel Prizes appeared.

2. Unselfish Reasoning Enhances Others

In 1904, Bessie Anderson Stanley composed the accompanying meaning of outcome in Earthy colored Book magazine:

He has made progress who has lived well, snickered frequently and cherished a lot; who has partaken in the trust of unadulterated ladies, the admiration of shrewd men and the adoration for young kids, who has filled his specialty and achieved his undertaking; who has left the world better than he tracked down it, whether by a superior poppy, an ideal sonnet, or a safeguarded soul; who has never needed enthusiasm for earth's magnificence or neglected to express it, who has consistently searched for the best in others and given them the best he had, whose life was a motivation, whose memory a beatitude.

At the point when you get beyond yourself and make a commitment to other people, you truly start to live.

3. Unselfish Reasoning Supports Different Ideals

At the point when you see a four-year-old, you hope to notice childishness. In any case, when you see it in a forty-year-old, it's not extremely alluring, right?

Of the relative multitude of characteristics an individual can seek after, unselfish reasoning appears to have the greatest effect toward developing different excellences. I feel that is on the grounds that the capacity to give unselfishly is so troublesome. It contradicts some common norms of human instinct. Yet, in the event that you can figure out how to think unselfishly and become a provider, then it becomes simpler to foster numerous different excellences: appreciation, love, regard, persistence, discipline, and so forth.

4. Unselfish Reasoning Expands Personal satisfaction

The soul of liberality made by unselfish reasoning gives individuals an appreciation forever and a comprehension of its higher qualities. Seeing those out of luck and providing for address that issue places a great deal of things into point of view. It builds the personal satisfaction of the provider and the recipient. That is the reason I trust that

- There is no life as vacant as the egotistical life.
- There is no life as focused as oneself void life.

To further develop your reality, then, at that point, concentrate on helping other people.

Merck and Company, the worldwide drug partnership, has consistently viewed itself as accomplishing more than just delivering items and creating a gain. It wants to serve mankind. During the 1980s, the organization created a medication to fix waterway visual impairment, a sickness that taints and causes visual impairment in large number of individuals, especially in emerging nations. While it was a decent item, potential clients couldn't bear to get it. So what did Merck do? It fostered the medication in any case, and in 1987 reported that it would give the medication free to anybody who required it. Starting around 1998, the organization had parted with in excess of 250 million tablets.

George W. According to merck, "We attempt never to fail to remember that medication is for individuals. It isn't for the benefits. The benefits follow, and assuming we have recalled that, they have never neglected to show up." The example to be learned? Basic. Rather than attempting to be perfect, be important for an option that could be more significant than yourself.

6. Unselfish Reasoning Makes a Heritage

Jack Balousek, president and head working official of Genuine North Interchanges, says, "Learn, procure, return — these are the three periods of life. The principal third ought to be dedicated to training, the second third to building a profession and getting by, and the last third to rewarding others — returning something in appreciation. Each state is by all accounts a groundwork for the following one."

In the event that you are effective, it becomes feasible for you to leave a legacy for other people. However, on the off chance that you want to accomplish more, to make a heritage, you really want to leave that in others. At the point when you think unselfishly and put resources into others, you gain the chance to make an inheritance that will outlast you.

Step by step instructions to EXPERIENCE THE Fulfillment OF UNSELFISH Reasoning

I think a great many people perceive the worth of unselfish reasoning, and most would try and concur that it's a capacity they might want to create. Many individuals, notwithstanding, are confused concerning how to transform their thought process. To start developing the capacity to think unselfishly, I suggest that you do the accompanying:

1. Put Others First

The interaction starts with understanding that everything isn't about you! That requires modesty and a change in center.

In The Force of Moral Oversee end, Ken Blanchard and Norman Vincent Peale expressed, "Individuals with modesty try not to think less about themselves; they simply think about themselves less." to turn out to be less childish in your thinking, then you want to quit pondering your needs and start zeroing in on others' necessities. Paul the Messenger urged, "Do nothing out of narrow minded aspiration or vain pride, yet in lowliness consider others better than yourselves. Every one of you ought to look not exclusively to your own advantages, yet additionally to the interests of others." 20 Sincerely promise to pay special attention to the interests of others.

2. Open Yourself to Circumstances Where Individuals Have Needs It's one thing to accept you will give unselfishly. It's one more to do it in fact. To make the progress, you want to set yourself in a position where you can see individuals' necessities and take care of business.

The sort of giving you do isn't significant from the beginning. You can serve at your congregation, make gifts to a food bank, volunteer proficient administrations, or provide for a beneficent association. The point is to figure out how to give and to develop the propensity for taking on a similar mindset as a provider.

3. Give Unobtrusively or Secretly

Whenever you have figured out how to give of yourself, then, at that point, the subsequent stage is to figure out how to give when you can't get anything consequently. It's quite often simpler to give when you get acknowledgment for it than it is the point at which nobody is probably going to be aware of it. Individuals who provide to get a great deal of show, in any case, have previously gotten any prize they will get. There are profound, mental, and close to home advantages that come exclusively to the people who give namelessly. Assuming you've never made it happen, attempt it.

4. Put resources into Individuals Purposefully

The most significant level of unselfish reasoning comes when you give of yourself to someone else for that individual's self-improvement or prosperity. On the off chance that you're hitched or a parent, you know this from individual experience. What does your mate esteem most exceptionally: cash in the bank or your time openly given? What might little kids actually rather have from you: a toy or your full focus? Individuals who love you would prefer to have you than what you can give them.

To turn into the sort of individual who puts resources into individuals, then, at that point, consider others and their excursion so you can team up with them. Every relationship resembles an organization made for common advantage. As you go into any relationship, contemplate how you can put resources into the other individual so it turns into a mutually beneficial arrangement. This is the way connections most frequently work out:

I win, you lose — I win just a single time.

You win, I lose — you win just a single time.

We both win — we win commonly.

We both lose — Farewell, association!

The best connections are mutual benefit. For what reason don't more individuals go into associations with that demeanor? I'll explain to you why: the vast majority need to ensure that they win first. Unselfish scholars, then again, go into a relationship and ensure that the other individual wins first. Furthermore, that has a significant effect.

5. Consistently Check Your 1otives

François de la Rochefoucauld said, "What is by all accounts liberality is in many cases something like masked desire, which ignores a little interest to get an incredible one." The hardest thing for a great many people is battling their normal inclination to put themselves first. That is the reason it's critical to constantly look at your thought processes to ensure you're not sliding in reverse into narrow-mindedness.

Would you like to actually look at your thought processes? Then, at that point, follow the displaying of Benjamin Franklin. Consistently, he posed himself two inquiries. At the point when he got up in the first part of the day, he would inquire, "What great am I going to do today?" And before he hit the hay, he would inquire, "What great have I done today?" In the event that you can respond to those inquiries with benevolence and trustworthiness, you can keep yourself on target.

GIVE WHILE YOU LIVE

In the fall of 2001, we as a whole seen an exhibit of unselfish reasoning dissimilar to anything we had found in the

US for a long time. Who can fail to remember the occasions of September 11, 2001? I had recently wrapped up educating an administration example when my associate, Linda Eggers, came into the studio to declare the grievous news. Like most Americans, I remained bolted to the TV the entire day and heard the reports of the firemen and police officials who hustled into the World Exchange Place pinnacles to help other people, never stressing over their own security.

Soon after the misfortune, a huge number of Americans communicated an extraordinary craving to accomplish something that would help what is going on. I had a similar longing. My organization was planned to do a preparation by means of simulcast on

September 15, the Saturday following the misfortune. Our initiative group chose to add a one-and-a-half-hour program named "America Implores" to the furthest limit of the simulcast. In it, my companion Max Lucado composed and read a request, communicating the heart's cry of millions. Franklin Graham petitioned God for our public chiefs. Jim and Shirley Dobson offered guidance to guardians on the best way to assist their kids with managing the occasion. Furthermore, Bruce Wilkinson and I asked the simulcast watchers to give monetarily to individuals harmed on September 11. Incredibly, they gave $5.9 million, which World Vision thoughtfully consented to disperse to those out of luck. Unselfish reasoning and giving turned a very dull hour into one of light and trust.

Under about fourteen days after the misfortune, I had the option to go to Ground Jerold in New York City. I went to see the site of the annihilation, to thank the people cleaning up the destruction, and to petition God for them. I can't actually do equity to what I saw. I've gone to New York many times. It's one of my number one spots in the world. My better half and I had been up in the pinnacles with our kids often previously and have awesome recollections of that area. To take a gander where the structures had once stood and to see only rubble, dust, and wound metal — it's basically unbelievable.

What numerous Americans didn't understand is that for the overwhelming majority months individuals worked determinedly to tidy up the site. Many were New York City firemen and other city laborers. Others were volunteers. They worked nonstop, seven days every week. Furthermore, when they went over the remaining parts of somebody in the rubble, they called for quiet and respectfully did them.

Since I'm a priest, I was approached to wear an administrative collar after entering the region. As I strolled around, numerous specialists saw the collar and requested that I petition God for them. It was a lowering honor.

American instructor Horace Mann said, "Be embarrassed to pass on until you have won some triumph for mankind." As per this norm, New York City's firemen are absolutely ready for death. The help they perform is many times really gallant. You and I might very well never be expected to set out our lives for other people, as they did. However, we can provide for others in various ways. We can be unselfish masterminds who put others first and enhance their lives. We can work with them so they go farther than they expected.

Thinking Question

Am I ceaselessly considering others and their process to think with greatest cooperation?

CHAPTER ELEVEN

DEPEND ON MAIN CONCERN THINKING

"There isn't no standards around here. We're attempting to achieve something."

How would you sort out the primary concern for your association, business, office, group, or gathering? In numerous organizations, the reality is in a real sense the main concern. Benefit decides if you are succeeding. However dollars shouldn't generally be the essential proportion of progress. Would you measure a definitive progress of your family by how much cash you had toward the month's end or year? What's more, on the off chance that you run a non-benefit or volunteer association, how might you know whether you were performing at your most noteworthy potential? How would you think main concern in that?

A NONPROFIT'S Main concern

Frances Hesselbein needed to ask herself precisely that inquiry in 1976, when she turned into the public chief overseer of the Young lady Scouts of America. At the point when she originally engaged with the Young lady Scouts, running the association was the last thing she anticipated. She and her better half, John, were accomplices in Hesselbein Studios, a little privately-run company that shot TV plugs and limited time films. She composed the contents and he made the movies. In the mid-1950s, she was selected as a worker troop pioneer at the Subsequent Presbyterian

Church in Johnstown, Pennsylvania. Indeed, even that was surprising, since she had a child and no little girls. Be that as it may, she consented to do it on a transitory premise. She probably adored it, since she drove the troop for a considerable length of time!

In time, she became gathering president and an individual from the public load up. Then, at that point, she filled in as chief head of the Bone Stone Young lady Scout Committee, a full-time paid position. When she accepted the position as Chief of the public association, the Young lady Scouts was in a difficult situation. The association needed course, young ladies were losing interest in exploring, and it was turning out to be progressively challenging to enroll grown-up volunteers, particularly with more prominent quantities of ladies entering the labor force. In the meantime, the Cub scouts was thinking about opening itself to young ladies. Hesselbein frantically expected to take the association back to the primary concern.

"We continued to pose ourselves exceptionally straightforward inquiries," she says. "What is our business? Who is our client? Also, what does the client think about esteem? In the event that you're the Young lady Scouts, IBM, or AT&T, you need to oversee for a mission." 21 Hesselbein's attention on mission empowered her to recognize the Young lady Scouts' primary concern. "We truly are here for one explanation: to assist a young lady with contacting her most elevated potential. More than any a certain something, that made the distinction. Since when you are clear about your main goal, corporate objectives and working targets stream from it."

When she sorted out her primary concern, she had the option to come up with a methodology to attempt to accomplish it. She began by redesigning the public staff. Then she made an arranging framework to be utilized by each of the 350 provincial chambers. Also, she acquainted administration preparing with the association. Hesselbein didn't limit herself to changes in authority and association. During the 1960s and '70s, the nation had changed thus had its young ladies

—however, the Young lady Scouts hadn't. Hesselbein handled that issue, as well. The association made its exercises more pertinent to the ongoing society, offering more noteworthy chances for utilization of PCs, for instance, as opposed to facilitating a get-together. She additionally searched out minority investment, made bilingual materials, and contacted low- pay families. On the off chance that assisting young ladies with arriving at their most elevated potential was the gathering's primary concern, why not be more forceful aiding young ladies who generally have less open doors? The procedure worked wonderfully.

Minority cooperation in the Young lady Scouts significantly increased.

In 1990, Hesselbein left the Young lady Scouts in the wake of making it a top of the line association. She proceeded to turn into the establishing president and Chief of the Peter F. Drucker Starting point for Philanthropic Administration, and presently fills in as administrator of its leading group of lead representatives. What's more, in 1998, she was granted the Official Award of Opportunity.

President Clinton said of Hesselbein during the function at the White House, "She has shared her astounding recipe for incorporation and greatness with endless associations whose primary concern is estimated not in dollars, however in changed lives." 23 He could never have said it better!

WHY YOU Ought to Partake in THE Arrival OF Primary concern THINKING

On the off chance that you're acclimated with thinking about the primary concern just as it connects with monetary issues, then, at that point, you might be missing a few things vital to you and your association. All things considered, consider the main concern the end, the focal point, the ideal outcome. Each movement has its own special main concern. In the event that you have some work, your work has a main concern. In the event that you serve in your congregation, your action has a main concern. So does your work as a parent, or companion, assuming you are one.

As you investigate the idea of primary concern thinking, perceive that it can help you in numerous ways:

1. Main concern Thinking Gives Incredible Clearness

What's the distinction among bowling and work? While bowling, it requires just three seconds to know how you've done indeed! That is one explanation individuals love sports to such an extent. There's no pausing and no speculating about the result.

Primary concern figuring makes it workable for you to gauge results all the more rapidly and without any problem. It gives you a benchmark by which to gauge action. It tends to be utilized as a zeroed in approach to guaranteeing that all your little exercises are deliberate and arrange to accomplish a bigger objective.

2. Primary concern Thinking Assists You with evaluating what is going on

At the point when you know your primary concern, it turns out to be a lot simpler to realize how you're doing in some random region.

At the point when Frances Hesselbein started running the Young lady Scouts, for instance, she measured everything against the association's objective of assisting a young lady with contacting her most noteworthy potential — from the association's administration structure (which she transformed from an order to a center) down to what identifications the young ladies could procure. There could be no more excellent estimation apparatus than the main concern.

3. Main concern Thinking Assists You with settling on the most ideal Choices

Choices become a lot more straightforward when you know your main concern. At the point when the Young lady Scouts were battling during the 1970s, outside associations attempted to persuade its individuals to turn into ladies' privileges activists or entryway to- entryway solicitors. In any case, under Hesselbein, it turned out to be simple for the Young lady Scouts to say no. It knew its main concern, and it needed to seek after its objectives with concentration and intensity.

4. Main concern Thinking Produces High Assurance

At the point when you know the primary concern and you pursue it, you incredibly increment your chances of winning. Furthermore, nothing creates high confidence like winning. How would you depict sports groups that bring home the title, or organization divisions that accomplish their objectives, or volunteers who accomplish their central goal? They're invigorated. Stirring things up around town feels invigorating. Furthermore, you can hit it provided that you understand what it is.

5. Main concern Thinking Guarantees Your Future

If you have any desire to find success tomorrow, you want to think main concern today. That is the very thing that Frances Hesselbein did, and she turned the Young lady Scouts around. Take a gander at any effective, enduring organization, and you'll find pioneers who know their primary concern. They go with their choices, allot their assets, enlist their kin, and construction their association to accomplish that main concern.

Instructions to Partake in THE Arrival OF Primary concern THINKING

Seeing the worth of the reality isn't hard. A great many people would concur that primary concern thinking has an exceptional yield. Yet, figuring out how to be a main concern scholar can challenge.

1. Distinguish the Genuine Primary concern

The course of main concern thinking starts with understanding what you're truly pursuing. It tends to be all around as elevated as the higher perspective vision, mission, or reason for an organization. Or then again it very well may be just about as engaged as what you need to achieve on a specific task. What's significant is that you be basically as unambiguous as could really be expected. Assuming that your objective is for something as unclear as "achievement," you will have a horrendously troublesome time attempting to bridle primary concern thinking to accomplish it.

The initial step is to save your "needs." Get to the outcomes you're truly searching for, the genuine quintessence of the objective. Put away any feelings that might cloud your judgment and eliminate any legislative issues that might impact your insight. What are you sincerely attempting to accomplish? At the point when you strip away everything that don't exactly make any difference, what are you constrained to accomplish? What should happen? What is adequate? That is the genuine primary concern.

2. Make the Main concern the Point

Have you at any point been in a discussion with somebody whose expectations appear to be other than expressed? Some of the time the circumstance reflects deliberate double dealing. However, it can likewise happen when the individual doesn't have the foggiest idea about his own baseline.

Exactly the same thing occurs in organizations. Some of the time, for instance, a hopefully expressed mission and the genuine primary concern don't correspond. Reason and benefits contend. Prior, I cited George W. Merck, who expressed, "We attempt never to fail to remember that medication is for individuals. It isn't for the benefits. The benefits follow, and assuming we have recalled that, they have never neglected to show up." He most likely offered that expression to remind those in his association that benefits self-reason — they don't contend with it.

In the event that creating a gain were the genuine primary concern, and aiding individuals just gave the necessary resources to accomplishing it, then the organization would endure. Its consideration would be isolated, and it would neither assistance individuals too as it could nor create as much gain as it wanted.

3. Make a Brilliant course of action to accomplish the Primary concern

Primary concern thinking accomplishes results. Hence, it normally follows that any plans that stream out of such thinking should tie straightforwardly to the reality — and there can be only one, not a few. When the reality not entirely set in stone, a methodology should be made to accomplish it. In associations, that frequently implies recognizing the center components or capabilities that should work appropriately to accomplish the main concern. This is the pioneer's obligation.

Significantly, when the main concern of every movement is accomplished, then THE reality is accomplished. On the off chance that the amount of the more modest objectives doesn't amount to the genuine main concern, then either your procedure is defective or you've not recognized your genuine main concern.

4. Adjust Colleagues to the Primary concern

When you have your methodology set up, ensure your kin line up with your technique. Preferably, all colleagues ought to know the major objective, as well as their singular job in accomplishing it. They need to know their own main concern and how that attempts to accomplish the association's main concern.

5. Stay with/ne Framework and Screen Results Ceaselessly

Dave Sutherland, a companion and previous leader of one of my organizations, accepts that a few associations cause problems by attempting to blend frameworks. He keeps up with that numerous sorts of frameworks can find success, however lending various frameworks or persistently changing starting with one then onto the next prompts disappointment. Dave says:

Main concern thinking can't be a one-time thing. It must be incorporated into the means of working and relating furthermore, accomplishing. Four can't simply tune into the ideal outcome from time to time. Accomplishing with primary concern thinking should be a lifestyle, or it will send inconsistent signals. I'm a main concern scholar. It is a section of my "framework" for accomplishment. I practice it consistently. No different estimations — no squandered endeavors.

Dave used to call individuals from his field group consistently to ask the primary concern inquiry they hope to hear. He constantly watched out for the organization's primary concern by observing it for each center region.

All things considered, no matter what your main concern, you can further develop it with very savvy. Furthermore, primary concern thinking has an extraordinary return since it assists with transforming your thoughts into results. Like no other sort of mental handling, it can assist you with harvesting the maximum capacity of your reasoning and accomplish anything that you want.

Thinking Question

Am I keeping fixed on the main concern with the goal that I can acquire the most extreme return and procure the maximum capacity of my reasoning?

One Last Thought

I trust you have partaken in this book. As you push ahead, I wish you achievement and propose that you keep in mind…

1. Everything starts with an idea.

"Life comprises of a's thought process day in and day out."

2. Our thought process figures out what our identity is. What our identity is figures out what we do.

"The activities of men are the best translators of their viewpoints."

3. Our contemplations decide our predetermination. Our predetermination decides our heritage.

"You are today where your considerations have brought you. You will be tomorrow where your contemplations take you."

4. Individuals who go to the top think uniquely in contrast to other people.

"Nothing limits accomplishment like little reasoning; Nothing grows conceivable outcomes like released thinking."

*. We can impact the manner in which we think.

"Anything things are valid… honorable… just… unadulterated… beautiful… are of good report. $f there is any prudence and assuming there is anything admirable; think on these things."

www.ingramcontent.com/pod-product-compliance
Lightning Source LLC
Chambersburg PA
CBHW052353220526
45465CB00003BA/1087